Contents

W9-ALV-904

Beyond the Zone System

Phil Davis

CURTIN & LONDON, INC.
Somerville, Massachusetts

VAN NOSTRAND REINHOLD CO.
New York Cincinnati Toronto Melbourne

Copyright © 1981 by Curtin & London, Inc.

All rights reserved. No part of this work covered by the copyright hereon may be reproduced or used in any form or by any means—graphic, electronic, or mechanical, including photocopying, recording, taping, or information storage and retrieval systems—without written permission of the publisher.

Printed in the United States of America

Published in 1981 by Curtin & London, Inc.
and Van Nostrand Reinhold Company
135 West 50th Street, New York NY 10020, U.S.A.

Van Nostrand Reinhold Limited
1410 Birchmount Road
Scarborough, Ontario M1P 2E7, Canada

Van Nostrand Reinhold Pty. Ltd.
17 Queen Street
Mitcham, Victoria 3132, Australia

Jacket design: Dianne Schaefer/Designworks
Jacket photograph: Dick Arentz
Interior design: Sharon Glassman
Chapter opening photographs: Dick Arentz
Illustrations: Laszlo Meszoly
Managing editor: Nancy Benjamin
Composition: The Heffernan Press
Printing and binding: Halliday Lithograph
Paper: 70# Patina matte, supplied by Lindenmeyr Paper Co.

10   9   8   7   6   5   4   3   2

Library of Congress Cataloging in Publication Data

Davis, Phil.
    Beyond the zone system.

    Includes index.
    1. Photography—Exposure.   2. Zone system
(Photography)   3. Photographic sensitometry.
I. Title.
TR591.D29   770'.28   81-530
ISBN 0-930764-23-4   AACR2
        0-930764-37-4 (pbk)

CHAPTER 12

Preface

It has taken me more than fifteen years to do the research and formulate the concepts and procedures that are presented in this book. Now that it's over and the problems have all been solved, I wonder why it took so long. There are no technical or theoretical discoveries here; the principles of sensitometry were established by Hurter and Driffield before 1890 and have been widely known and used—at least in industry—for decades. I've done little more than interpret those principles, with somewhat altered emphasis, so that they can be applied to the solution of practical photographic problems.

I have no intention of re-igniting the art-vs.-science controversy that's been smouldering ever since H. P. Robinson denounced Hurter and Driffield's work in the 1890s, but, whether we wish to admit it or not, photography—even art photography—is based on scientific principles. The processes are predictable, controllable, and governed by physical laws. I believe that a photographer who understands these principles, and applies them, can work more efficiently and with greater artistic freedom than one who merely follows instructions.

I hope this book will contribute to your understanding and that you'll find the procedures useful. In studying this book I hope you'll also share some of my enthusiasm as, after the initial confusion has abated, the puzzle pieces begin to fit into place and you gradually perceive the order and elegance of the process relationships.

I'm considerably indebted to the hundreds of students who have unwittingly served as a test panel for my theories as they evolved. Their interest and excitement has encouraged me in these investigations and convinced me that the approach is both sound and practical. I'm also grateful to a number of friends and colleagues who have challenged me and provided inspiration; among them, Bill Rauhauser, Dick Stevens, and Dick Arentz.

I'm thankful for advice and direction I received from Carl Shipman and Ted DiSante in the early stages of this project. Michael Simon graciously read the manuscript and offered a number of helpful suggestions. Hollis Todd's critical review was both encouraging and valuable. My thanks, too, to Dick Zakia for his interest and support.

I'm grateful to David Vestal for generously sharing his own research findings with me; also to Bob Schwalberg, whose critical analysis of and personal interest in my procedures are much appreciated. Bob Routh deserves special thanks for his enthusiastic support and his unstinting efforts in organizing workshops and spreading the gospel of sensitometry-for-the-masses. I'm indebted to Richard Shaper, Quantum Instruments Inc., for his cooperation and interest in lending me items for testing, and supplying technical information; also to Tom Perazella, Berkey Marketing Companies, for arranging equipment loans and for his personal interest and consultation.

I must acknowledge my wife's contributions with loving gratitude; without Martha's interest, encouragement, typing skills, and limitless patience, this book might never have been completed. Finally, to Nancy Benjamin, managing editor, whose patience I have sorely tried on more than one occasion; and to Denny Curtin, publisher and friend, whose interest in this project impelled him—incredibly—to attend one of my workshops, my sincere thanks for performance above and beyond the call of duty.

CHAPTER
1

Why Sensitometry?

Photography has many faces. It can record scientific data, stimulate sales, document news events, provide calendar illustrations, and keep family memories alive. It's a vital tool, serving some practical purpose in almost every area of our society. It's one of the most engrossing and rewarding hobbies imaginable. It's also the most widely practiced and popular art form in history.

Everyone, it seems, is a photographer. Modern automated cameras are virtually foolproof; modern films are sensitive enough to record satisfactory images in almost any light condition, and commercial processors can provide overnight service. It's no wonder photography is considered an easy medium. Anyone who can point and shoot can have photographs.

But photography isn't that simple. It only seems that way because scientists and designers have worked for years to protect us from any sort of technical unpleasantness. They've devised products and processes of incredible complexity—functional and reliable enough, but mysterious in their workings. We can marvel at the miracle of instant color pictures—automatically focused and exposed—which develop in daylight before our eyes, but we're barred from participating in the photographic part of the miracle itself. We can contribute only after the fact, and in a limited way, by dissecting or manipulating the packaged image as the camera delivers it.

In this extreme example, technology provides the product but insulates us from the process. On the other extreme, technicians who supervise the development of color film in a commercial laboratory must be concerned with the process alone; they are denied a product in the usual sense. Most of us are not content to settle for either extreme. The automatically produced picture is depersonalized and cheapened by the ease of its creation, and the control of process for its own sake strikes most of us as drudgery. It's human nature to measure success by the difficulty of its achievement, but it's also important to have some tangible symbol of that success for others to recognize and admire.

In the past, photography was much more dependent on craftsmanship than it is today. Our photographic ancestors were capable of making their own plates and papers almost from scratch. Using only a silver dollar, some nitric acid, an egg or two, a little salt, and a sheet of paper, they could be making prints in a few hours' time. They weren't limited to silver, either. They made photographs with platinum, dye, ink, crushed rose petals, carbon and other things—none of which came in the familiar yellow box. They were an ingenious, persistent, durable lot because they had to be. Skillful photographers got good results; inept ones didn't.

Craftsmanship and skill are revered somewhat less today but we still recognize the superior technique of people like Ansel Adams and Minor White. This is especially true when the image itself is interesting or evocative. The most memorable photographs seem to combine form and content in mutual dependence.

Not all memorable photographs resemble Adams' or White's, of course. Technical excellence doesn't necessarily imply a full tonal scale, needle-sharp focus, and a grainless image. Good technique is

Minor White, "Moon and Wall Encrustations." Courtesy of The Minor White Archive, Princeton University, copyright © The Trustees of Princeton University.

4

whatever is appropriate to the content: harsh and grainy in the case of Bill Brandt's nudes; soft and muted in the case of Marie Consindas' early Polacolor still-life compositions; stark and pale, as Avedon's portraits of his dying father. Think about the photographs you've admired. It's unlikely that any of them are technically poor. Almost without exception, the photographers we respect achieve a nice balance between art and craft.

You can't learn to be a great photographer simply by reading; but books can teach you how the photographic process works and how to control it. Then it's up to you to put that knowledge to work. With practice and experience you can master the craft and add a new dimension of technical excellence to your photographs.

I hope this book will help. It covers black-and-white processes

Richard E. Arentz

Thomas R. Drew

only, and relates particularly to large-format cameras that use sheet film. This limited approach was chosen because sheet film can be processed one sheet at a time, if need be, permitting individual control of image quality. Rollfilm and 35mm users will find a great deal of pertinent information here, but will not be able to apply the actual control procedures very easily or effectively.

Unlike most instructional books on the market, this one advocates the use of sensitometric procedures for testing materials and deriving useful working information. This has never been a popular approach to the subject for two reasons: sensitometry suggests laboratory science, with its frightening emphasis on mathematics; also, sensitometry requires the use of a densitometer—an instrument that is typically very expensive and rarely available to the nonprofessional photographer. I hope you'll discover, in the following chapters, that both of these problems have been satisfactorily resolved. I think you'll find the math much less fearsome than it's reputed to be, and, in the accompanying

Workbook, you'll find complete plans and instructions for building simple, inexpensive, and completely practical densitometers.

Compared with the usual trial-and-error approach to materials testing, sensitometry has numerous advantages. First, it's standard industry procedure, so the published literature can be related to your own work. Second, it's objective and efficient; human judgment is replaced by measurement, and the test results are displayed in economical graphic form. Third, the procedures provide much more data—and more accurate data—than can be discovered by trial-and-error. Fourth, it's actually quite easy and there's a considerable saving in time and materials. Fifth, it will add to your knowledge of the photographic process and suggest new ways of manipulating or controlling the image for your personal creative purposes. Finally, contrary to a common prejudice, sensitometry does *not* impose any technical restraints on your creative efforts. It simply provides you with information; you can use that information in any way that suits you.

The text begins with a general review of the nature of the black-and-white photographic process. An explanation of sensitometric principles follows and the test and analysis procedures are thoroughly explained and illustrated. Then the test data are applied to actual photographic practice and three methods of exposure-development control are described. Suggestions for troubleshooting and personalizing the procedures conclude the text. A brief glossary provides definitions of technical terms. A Workbook is available to accompany *Beyond the Zone System,* and has been designed to simplify the application of the exposure and development systems described in this book. The Workbook includes complete plans, cutout parts, and a high-quality reproduction of the 21-zone fan scale used to construct your own Wonder Wheel. It also includes plans and step-by-step instructions for adapting your Luna-Pro meter as a reflection densitometer and your Pentax or Minolta spotmeter as reflection *and* transmission densitometers. Also included are graphs on which to record testing data and exposure logs on which to record exposure and development information.

If this sounds formidable it's because we're facing the issue head on. Photography is a highly technical medium but, for that very reason, highly controllable. Every time you trip the shutter or immerse the film in the developer, you can be sure the process is doing something. You'll be a more competent and more confident photographer if you know what it's doing—and what it will do next—so you can stay in control.

So carry on. You may find it rough going in spots but give it a good try. Like taking a cold shower, it may be a little difficult to get into, and may not be entirely enjoyable while you're in it—but you'll feel really great when it's over!

Learning the Language

Exposing film to light produces a latent image which can be made visible by chemical development. Similarly, printing paper, suitably exposed, forms a latent image which appears in a few seconds when the paper is immersed in the developer solution.

In both cases the visible image is composed of masses of tiny particles of silver. Because the black silver deposit forms most densely where the exposing light was most intense, the film image records the highlights as dark tones and the shadows as light-toned, transparent grays. The film image is called a *negative* because of this tone reversal.

Tone reversal occurs whenever a silver emulsion is exposed and developed (a few special emulsions are exceptions to this rule). Therefore, the print image is really a negative-of-the-negative, or *positive*, and its tonality is similar to that of the original subject.

If both film and printing paper are given optimum exposure and development, the print will not only record the subject, but will also display its tones, from light to dark, in satisfactory relationship. The subtleties of highlight and shadow will be evident, and the print may become a beautiful object in its own right. If significant errors occur in either process, the print image will probably be less than satisfactory. If the subject brightness and contrast are not estimated correctly, the film may not record an image of optimum quality. If the exposure and development of either film or paper are incorrect, the print image may turn out to be too flat (low contrast) or too contrasty, too light or too dark, and detail rendering and tone gradation will probably suffer.

Although exposure and development are somewhat interdependent, it's possible to draw some conclusions about their separate effects. In general terms, film exposure controls the density of the negative and development controls contrast; that is, overexposure (with standardized development) will produce a dense negative which will appear dark in tone. Underexposure will yield a low-density negative which will appear pale and light in tone. If exposure is standardized and development is varied, film will react to overdevelopment by

These negatives, photographed on a light box, show the effects of variation in film exposure and development. The top row represents a 2-stop overexposure; the middle row normal exposure; the bottom row a 2-stop underexposure. The left column represents one-half normal developing time; the middle column normal developing time; the right column twice-normal developing time.

producing a negative image of higher-than-normal contrast; underdevelopment will leave the image flat (low in contrast) and weakly gray.

Papers don't react to development variations quite so obviously. Underdevelopment, if severe enough to produce any obvious effect, is likely to result in weak, mottled, brownish-gray print tones, which some people refer to as "muddy." Extending print development doesn't have any dramatic effect on image contrast, but gradation will change and the image will darken overall as development proceeds. If greatly overdeveloped, the print is likely to show signs of fog (grayed highlights) or stains.

Papers react to exposure variations, just as films do, with even more obvious results. Underexposure will result in a lighter-than-normal print with possible loss of highlight details. Overexposure will darken the image and may obscure shadow details. You can establish some control over these variables by careful empirical testing—which is another way of saying "try it and see if it works." This is a good way for beginners to work, but after you've become more expert it helps to know some theory. Theory can accelerate the learning process considerably, but it can be tiresome if it's not related to practice. A middle ground is best. We'll use sensitometry—the scientific analysis of exposure and development—to compile working data for use in the field.

What the Numbers Mean

If you're new to sensitometry, words like *graphs, geometric,* and *densitometer* may be scary. If you conscientiously avoided math in school and have since tried to forget the little you learned, join the group. Very few adults—especially visual types—feel comfortable with

numbers of any sort, with the possible exception of football scores and lottery numbers.

Don't worry. You won't have to do much computing, other than some simple arithmetic, to handle the numbers in sensitometry. You don't even have to know what the numbers *mean* in some cases. Think of them as a kind of shorthand, used to simplify and demonstrate relationships that would be more difficult to explain in words.

Actually, you probably know more about numbers than you think

This series illustrates the effect of variation in print developing time. Exposure was the same (5 seconds) for all the prints. Print 1 was developed for 30 seconds; print 2 for 1 minute; print 3 for 2 minutes; print 4 for 4 minutes; print 5 for 6 minutes; and print 6 for 8 minutes.

you do. Whether you realize it or not, you use numbers in some way every day. You can't go shopping, balance your checkbook, bake a cake, or tune the television set without using numbers and, if you've ever done a crossword puzzle or played bingo (Fig. 2-1), you've had some experience with the principles of graphic representation. Although the numbers and graphs you're about to encounter may seem strange and formidable, the only thing you have to fear is fear itself.

Arithmetic Series

Many of the numbers you use in photography occur in series. For example, the numbers on the frame counter of a 35mm camera—1, 2, 3, 4, 5, etc.—are in what is known as an *arithmetic series*. This means that the number sequence can be formed or extended by *addition* or *subtraction*. It's obvious, in this case, that the series can be extended by adding or subtracting 1. For example, the number following 22 is 23—found by adding 1 to 22. Similarly, the number before 17 is 16—17 minus 1. The number 1 in this sequence is called a *constant* because it remains unchanged throughout the series and can be applied to any number in the series to find the next one.

The constant in a series can be any number. For example, when making a test strip to determine optimum print exposure you might set the timer on 5 and push the button repeatedly to produce this arithmetic series of exposures:

$$5, 10, 15, 20, 25, 30$$

and so on. In this case, obviously, the constant is 5.

Geometric Series

Most number sequences in photography are *geometric* series, formed by *multiplication* or *division* by a constant. Shutter speeds are a familiar example of a geometric series employing the constant 2. Almost all modern cameras, with the exception of some fully automatic types, display this sequence of shutter speeds:

$$1, 2, 4, 8, 15, 30, 60, 125, 250, 500, 1000$$

Older cameras may use a slightly different sequence:

$$1, 2, 5, 10, 25, 50, 100, 250, 500, 1000$$

or, in some cases:

$$1, 2, 5, 10, 25, 50, 100, 200, 400$$

In each case the sequences progress by multiples of 2, at least approximately.

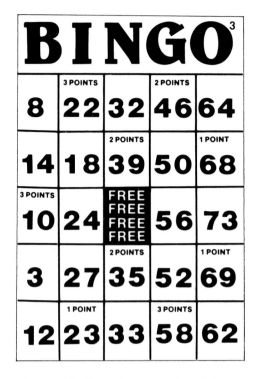

Figure 2-1. If you've ever played Bingo you've worked with a simple graph. The letters B, I, N, G, O identify the vertical columns of numbers. The individual numbers locate points in each column. Each letter-number combination describes one—and only one—square on the card. (Bingo Card courtesy of the Warren Paper Company.)

Camera exposures are counted in an arithmetic series.

Because the shutter speed series is based on the constant 2, moving from one number to the next will either double or halve the previous exposure. For example, changing from 8 (1/8 second) to 15 (1/15 second) cuts the exposure in half; going from 8 (1/8) to 4 (1/4) doubles it. The newer speed sequence is more nearly accurate in this respect than the older, but neither is precise: 1/15 is not exactly half of 1/8, nor is 1/60 just twice as long a time as 1/125. These slight inaccuracies, however, are negligible.

Two other familiar examples of geometric progression are the series of aperture numbers, or f-numbers, and the ASA film speed series. The standard sequence of f-numbers goes like this:

f/ 1, 1.4, 2, 2.8, 4, 5.6, 8, 11, 16, 22, 32, etc.

The constant in this series is not immediately obvious; notice, however, that every *second* number in the series is doubled. In any such sequence the constant is the *square root of 2,* or about 1.41.

These shutter speeds are in an imprecise geometric sequence whose constant is approximately 2.

ASA

If every *third* number is doubled, the constant is the *cube root of 2,* or about 1.26. This is the basis for the familiar ASA film speed series:

10, 12, 16, 20, 25, 32, 40, 50, 64, 80, 100, 125, 160, 200, etc.

The new ISO (International Organization for Standardization) film speeds are based on the same interval. These numbers are approximate, of course. The precise values would be unwieldy.

Lens f-numbers progress in a geometric series whose constant is about 1.41.

Steps and Stops

Although the term *stop* originally referred to the lens aperture itself, its meaning now commonly applies to almost any influence that changes exposure by a factor of 2. We call the aperture a stop and talk about *stopping down* to smaller apertures. However, we don't *stop up;* we *open up* a lens when we change to a larger aperture.

Although a change in shutter speed has no effect at all on light intensity, it is sometimes described as affecting the exposure "a stop or two." When the sun goes behind a cloud, we say the light has dropped "a couple of stops." A filter may have a "three-stop factor"—meaning it requires an exposure increase of 8×—and we may even compare one film with another as "a stop slower."

Some authorities claim that the term *stop* should be used to refer exclusively to aperture adjustments, and they prefer the term *step* to describe doubled or halved exposures. Despite this, the term *stop* will be used almost exclusively in this book for two reasons: first, it is universally understood and commonly used; second, it is frequently necessary to refer to *steps* of exposure that are not *stops.* For example, the steps of a test strip don't necessarily progress by a factor of 2, and the familiar *step tablet*, which we'll refer to frequently, should really be called a "half-step tablet," since its density steps progress in half-stop increments. Remember, in this book, when *step* is used, it will describe a discrete increment of exposure or density in a series, without any implication of value. In other words, the difference between one step and the next may be one or more stops or some fraction of a stop, depending on the circumstances.

When the term is used to refer to exposure, a change of one stop is understood to imply doubling or halving of the previous value. Thus, increasing a camera exposure setting of, say, 1/8 sec. at f/16 by 3 stops, might be done by multiplying the exposure time by 2, three times (1/8 × 2 = 1/4 × 2 = 1/2 × 2 = 1 second) or by opening the lens up 3 stops (from f/16 to f/11 to f/8 to f/5.6) or by some combination of these adjustments, such as, for example 1/4 sec. at f/8.

For comparison, this is the way stops relate to the other series mentioned previously:

Stops:	1	2	3	4
Shutter speeds:	1/125	1/60	1/30	1/15	1/8
f-numbers:	16	11	8	5.6	4
ASA film speeds:	10 12 16 20 25 32 40 50 64 80 100 125 160

Although these scales are not intended to represent equivalent *values*, from left to right they all represent increasing exposure. For example, exchanging a film of ASA 10 for one of ASA 40 will increase the exposure effect 2 stops, as will a change in shutter speed from, say, 1/60 to 1/15, or a change in aperture from f/8 to f/4. Notice in this comparison that the normal shutter speed sequence and aperture number sequence both change in full-stop increments; that is, each new number represents a full-stop change in exposure. The ASA numbers, by comparison, progress in one-third stop increments—a convenience you'll appreciate later on.

It's sometimes convenient in discussing exposure sequences to consider all the possible influences together as a total exposure effect. For example, if a subject is illuminated by 400 foot-candles and reflects 30% of the light toward the camera, and if the lens admits 10% of that light and the shutter allows it to act on film of ASA 400 for 1/60 sec., it's convenient to consider that the film has received "one unit" of exposure. Then, if something changes—if we alter the shutter speed to 1/30 sec., for example—we can say the film has received "two units" and the change is easily understood. We frequently work this way, with relative values of exposure, because it often doesn't matter *why* the exposure changes, but it is important to know *how much* it changes.

The effect of exposure change is geometric rather than arithmetic, and the actual numbers are of little significance compared to their ratio. For example, if you vary exposures in an arithmetic sequence—as some people do when making test strips—the effect of the exposure increases will diminish as the series progresses. In this arithmetic series of exposure times, for example:

$$1, 2, 3, 4, 5, 6, 7, 8, 9, 10, \text{etc.}$$

the change from 1 (unit) to 2 is a full stop; the exposure has been doubled and the effect on the image will probably be obvious. The change from 4 to 5, however, represents an increase of only 25% and the change from 9 to 10 increases the exposure only about 11%. These changes will have a relatively insignificant effect on the film or paper emulsion and the resulting image density changes may not be visible.

An arithmetic test strip. Contrast is high between the first few steps but decreases as the sequence progresses.

To achieve a uniform rate of increase we need to use a geometric series of exposures. If full stop increases are desired, the constant must be 2:

$$1, 2, 4, 8, 16, 32, 64, 128, 256, \text{etc.}$$

If less drastic—but still uniform—steps are wanted, the constant can be less than 2, perhaps 1.5:

$$1, 1.5, 2.25, 3.38, 5.07, 7.6, 11.4, 17.1, \text{etc.}$$

A geometric sequence of test exposures, based on the constant 1.5. All the steps are clearly visible.

Usually we work with full-stop increments of exposure change and, because we frequently encounter ranges of 10 or more stops, the numbers themselves can become unwieldy. A 10-stop range (subject luminance range, as measured with a meter) represents an exposure ratio of 1:1028, for example, and 15 stops covers a range of about 1:32,000! Often the numbers, per se, are unimportant, which is one reason we use the word *stop* so frequently; it implies a change of known magnitude and has equal significance at all values of exposure.

The term *stop* is especially useful in discussing camera exposures. It is less appropriate (but sometimes employed carelessly) for descriptions of negative or print characteristics. We can be much more specific in analyzing the finished image, whether on film or paper, and it's more important to know the actual values of image density and contrast. Here again the geometric values of exposure and density are significant, but unwieldy. To simplify things we resort to a kind of numerical shorthand—*logarithms*. Don't panic, now, they're friendly!

Logarithms: Numerical Shorthand

There are several kinds of logarithms but we'll be concerned only with the so-called *common logs*, or *logs to the base ten*. In this system the number *10* is the basic building block from which all other numbers can be derived and the log of a number represents the number of times 1 must be multiplied by *10* to produce the number. For example, 1 must be multiplied by 10 *once* to make 10, so the log of 10 is 1. To make 100, you must multiply 1 by 10 *twice*, so the log of 100 is 2. The log number 3 indicates that 3 10's were multiplied, and the number they represent is, therefore, 1000. The number 3 in this example is called the *log* of 1000; 1000 is called the *antilog* of 3.

Another way of expressing this relationship is to define a log as a *power* of 10. You are undoubtedly familiar with numbers like 10^2 (ten squared) or 10^3 (ten cubed). You can also call them *ten to the second power* or *ten to the third power*. In these examples, the numbers 2 and 3 are called *exponents* as well as *powers*, so the log of a number is really the exponent, or power, of 10 required to produce the number.

The logs of even multiples of 10 are easy to determine and quite obvious. The number 100,000 requires 5 10's (count the zeroes) and can be written as $10 \times 10 \times 10 \times 10 \times 10 = 100,000$, or as 10^5. More simply still, written as a logarithm, the number is 5. Remember, in this system every log number is the exponent of 10, but the 10 is not written. The log number 4, then, means 10^4 and equals 10,000; 7 means 10^7 and equals 10,000,000. You'll appreciate the obvious simplification provided by logarithms when dealing with large numbers.

The logs of most numbers are not quite so easy to determine. Tables of logarithms are available in math books but these days we usually use calculators to find them. You can get along quite nicely in sensitometry without a calculator, but you'll find one useful. If you plan to buy one, get a model that provides *log, reciprocal,* and *power* functions; they'll be listed in the specifications as *log, 1/x* and Y^x

functions. Usually calculators that provide these functions are called *scientific* or *slide-rule* calculators. You can get one adequate for your needs in sensitometry for less than twenty dollars.

Whether or not you have a calculator, you'll soon learn a few logs by heart. You'll also learn to find most of the others you need by counting on your fingers and using simple arithmetic.

Probably the most useful log number is *0.3*. It's the log of *2*, and it's important because it's equivalent to a stop. It's easy, therefore, to convert stops to logs and logs to stops. Simply multiply stops by 0.3 to find the log range and, to find stops, divide the log range by 0.3. For example, an exposure range of 7 stops is equivalent to (the log number) 2.1 (7 × 0.3 = 2.1); and—working the other way—1.4 equals 4 2/3 stops (1.4 ÷ 0.3 = 4.666).

It's only slightly more complicated to translate exposure ratios into log numbers. If you have a calculator, the log representing a ratio of 1:256, for example, is found by simply punching *256*, then the log key, and the answer is immediate: 2.40824. This is more nearly precise than necessary; 2.4 will do for our purposes. To find the log without a calculator, convert the ratio to stops by counting on your fingers:

1:2	=	1 stop
1:4	=	2 stops
1:8	=	3 stops
1:16	=	4 stops
1:32	=	5 stops
1:64	=	6 stops
1:128	=	7 stops
1:256	=	8 stops

then, 8 (stops) × 0.3 = 2.4

By similar calculation and estimation you can find most of the log equivalents you need.

An inexpensive calculator suitable for use with the procedures outlined in this book. The display reads 3.0103 −01, which is the $\log_{10}$ of 2 as it is written in "scientific notation." The final two digits, −01, indicate that the decimal point must be moved one space to the left. The actual value of the number displayed is .30103.

One of the most interesting features of log numbers is that *adding* them is equivalent to *multiplying* their *antilogs*. For example, the log of 10 is 1 and the log of 100 is 2. Adding 1 + 2 = 3, the log of 1000, which is also the product of the antilogs, 10 × 100. Use the reverse procedure to divide. For example, what is 100,000 divided by 100? Subtract 2 (the log of 100) from 5 (the log of 100,000) and you get 3. The antilog of 3 is 1000. This is a simple case but the principle holds for more complex numbers.

If you don't want to buy a calculator, you can get along comfortably with the list of logs and antilogs in the Workbook, page 50. You'll notice the list of logs progresses in units of 0.05 (equivalent to 1/6 stop), which is close enough for all but the most exacting calculations in sensitometry.

Graphs and Charts

In working with sensitometry, you'll have to work with numbers, of course, but the worst is over as soon as you feel friendly toward logs. Actually, you won't have to do much mathematical calculation of any sort because most of the data we'll be working with will be displayed in the form of graphs or charts. Let's review some principles about graphs.

Graphs, in their various forms, give us a way to compare two or more quantities visually. This makes the relationships less abstract than they would be in verbal or numerical form and easier to grasp intuitively. You've undoubtedly seen area, bar, and line graphs in advertisements and news magazines; they are used to compare, for example, the relative amounts of tar in cigarette brands, trace the course of inflation, or illustrate the statistics of population growth.

Area graphs—the pie graph is a familiar example—are good for comparing relative quantities, such as oil reserves, nuclear missiles, and portions of the national budget spent on armaments, welfare, etc.

Bar graphs are excellent for displaying data that change with time and thus can be used to suggest trends. For example, suppose you want to keep track of the barometric pressure fluctuations during a three-day period. By consulting your barometer at regular intervals you may assemble the following data:

Day	Hour	Pressure
Monday	12:01 A.M.	30.33
	8:00 A.M.	30.12
	4:00 P.M.	30.03
	Midnight	30.00
Tuesday	8:00 A.M.	29.80
	4:00 P.M.	29.74
	Midnight	29.91
Wednesday	8:00 A.M.	30.13
	4:00 P.M.	30.23
	Midnight	30.30

By plotting time on the horizontal axis (also called the x-axis) against pressure on the vertical axis (also called the y-axis), you can produce a bar graph that looks like Figure 2-2. This presentation allows comparison of the known data points and suggests the change of pressure that occurs with time. It is even more informative if the data points are connected to imply that the pressure change is *continuous*. In Figure 2-3a, the points have been connected to form a line graph but here the jagged quality of the line implies that the barometric pressure changes were abrupt and unsubtle. Since we know that's not the case, we can produce a more appropriate indication by rounding off the jagged points and softening the contours of the line (Fig. 2-3b).

In Figure 2-4 this adjusted contour is compared with the actual trace from a recording barometer (in the barometer trace the y-axis is curved to coincide with the arc of the recording pen arm but this doesn't affect the data in any way). In these illustrations it's apparent that the line graph would be more accurate if more data points were

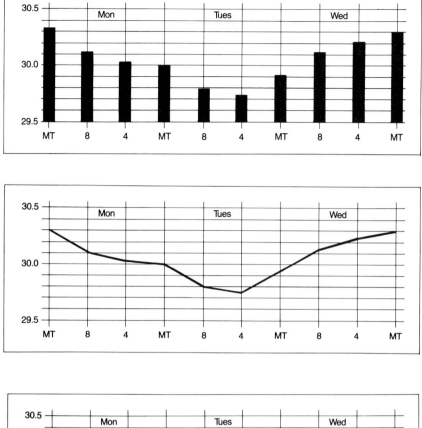

Figure 2-2. The x-axis of this bar graph is calibrated in time (days and hours) and the y-axis is calibrated in pressure (inches of mercury). The bars indicate by their height the barometric pressure that existed at specific 8-hour intervals over a three-day period.

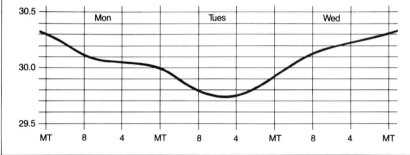

Figure 2-3a. Here the tips of the bars have been connected with straight lines (and the bars erased) to suggest the trend of barometric pressure change.

Figure 2-3b. Since pressure changes gradually, the trend is shown more realistically with this smoothly curved line. From this line you can estimate the pressure that existed at any time between the calibration points.

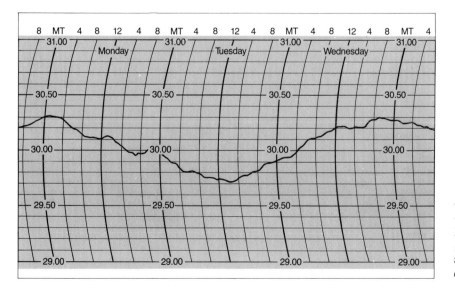

Figure 2-4. Here is a barometer trace showing the minute-by-minute changes in pressure. Even though the line graph (2-3b) was drawn from only 10 widely spaced data points, it approximates the actual curve quite well.

19

used, but the trend of pressure variations is discernible and it's possible to estimate with reasonable accuracy the pressures that existed at odd hours between the given reference points.

If you are confident that you understand the principles of math and graphic presentation covered in this chapter, you're ready to work with photographic problems. If not, I suggest you review the material until you're more at ease with it. To test yourself, work through the sample exercises and check your results on pp. 181-82.

Test Exercises

1. You find an old lens in a camera shop. The aperture scale is marked with these numbers: f/6.3, 9, 12.7, 18, 25, 36. There are two more marks but the numbers are illegible. What are they?

2. You have a red filter with a factor of 8×. If your exposure is correct at f/16 without the filter, what aperture should you use when the filter is in use?

3. In taking meter readings of your subject you discover that the highlights are 8 stops brighter than the shadows. What is the luminance ratio (brightness range)?

4. You are printing and want to make a geometric test strip, but doubling the exposure makes the steps too abrupt. Beginning with an exposure time of 2 seconds, what times can you use if you want to produce eight steps, increasing by half-stop intervals? What is the constant in this series?

5. The ISO film speeds combine the old ASA (geometric) and DIN (logarithmic) numbers so that a film such as Plus-X, which formerly had an ASA rating of 125 and a DIN rating of 22, is now rated at ISO 125/22°, and Tri-X professional film is now rated ISO 320/26°. A friend gives you a roll of German film marked DIN 21; what is its ISO rating?

6. Neutral density filters (ND filters) are gray in color and are used to reduce light intensity in accurately calibrated amounts. Their factors are logarithmic; that is, an ND 0.3 filter reduces light intensity by 1 stop. If you need to reduce your camera exposure by 100 times, what ND filter should you use?

7. You are taking a picture for which motion and depth-of-field requirements demand a shutter speed of 1 sec. and a lens opening of f/8. With the film in use and the existing light conditions, your meter tells you the exposure should be 1 sec. at f/45. By how many stops must the light intensity be reduced? What value of ND filtration will be required to permit your desired camera settings?

8. If a single ND 0.3 filter reduces 1000 units of light to 500 units, how many units of light will pass through if you add an ND 1.0 to make a total of 1.3?

9. If you need to reduce 2000 units of light to 5 units, what value of ND filtration must you provide?

10. Plot these values on the graph provided (Fig. 2-5).

Contrast Index (y-axis)	Minutes Developing Time (x-axis)
0.3	0.8
0.4	1.5
0.5	2.65
0.6	4.7
0.7	9.25

Figure 2-5.

How long must you develop to reach a contrast index of 0.45? If you develop for three minutes, approximately what contrast index do you attain?

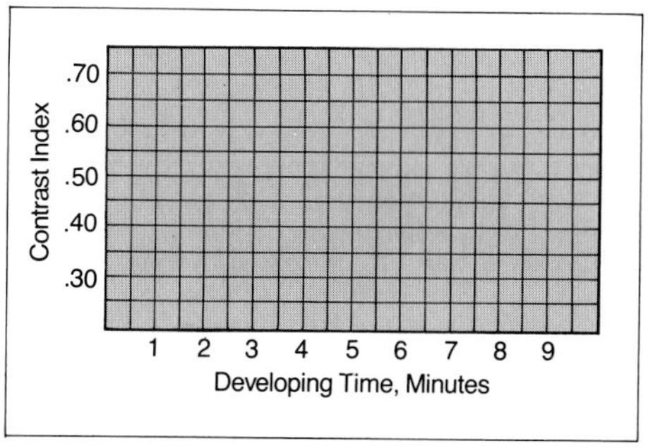

CHAPTER
3

How to Read
and Interpret
Film Curves

Line graphs are used almost exclusively in photography because they "fill in" gaps between known data points, providing new information and indicating trends. Figure 3-1 is a typical line graph which shows the relationship between film exposure, film development, and the resulting image density (darkness). These graph data lines are called *characteristic curves* (or H & D curves, after Hurter and Driffield, who devised them in the 1880s).

The formal arrangement of these characteristic curve graphs is standardized. Values of log exposure are always displayed along the (horizontal) x-axis, increasing from left to right. Values of image density are always displayed along the (vertical) y-axis, increasing from bottom to top. The calibration units on the two axes are always in the same *scale*, although not always in the same numerical system.

Some Terms Defined

Exposure values on the graphs you'll encounter refer to the combined effect of light intensity and time. The standard exposure unit is called the *meter-candle-second* (mcs) and one mcs is the exposure that a film will receive if a "standard candle" is held one meter from the film surface for one second. (Today, the "standard candle" is a carefully regulated electric light, which relates to the intensity of solidifying molten platinum rather than to burning wax.) You may see references to the *lux-second* instead of the mcs. The terms, for all practical purposes, are interchangeable.

You may occasionally see the exposure axis of a graph calibrated in mcs or other units of this sort but usually the values are converted to logs, identified as *log E* or *log H* values—both of which mean *log exposure*.

Frequently you'll see exposure values labelled *relative log E*. This simply means that the numbers are in correct proportion but are not the

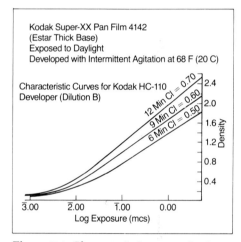

Figure 3-1. *Characteristic curves for Super XX sheet film developed in HC-110B.* © Eastman Kodak Company, 1976

actual exposure values. Any one of several reasons may account for this: the actual exposure may not be known; the graph may represent a hypothetical film, or a class of films for which no single exposure series would be appropriate; or the graph may be based on some nonstandard exposure test, such as varied shutter speeds, which can't be expressed in mcs. Most of the graphs you'll see in this book—and all that you make yourself—will be calibrated in relative values, which is a perfectly respectable way to work.

The term *density* has a special meaning. By definition, *density* is the common log of opacity which, in turn, is the reciprocal of *transmittance*. Want to go over that again?

Transmittance is the ability of a material to allow light to pass through it; it is usually expressed as a fraction or a percentage—what comes out divided by what went in. Opacity is just the opposite. It refers to a material's ability to block or absorb light and is expressed in ordinary numbers, never less than 1. *Density*, to repeat, is the log of opacity, and is sometimes written as log o or $\log_{10} o$.

As an example, suppose some material can transmit 25% of the light that strikes it; 25% is equivalent to the fraction ¼, the reciprocal of which is 4. The opacity of the material is, therefore, 4, and the density is the log of 4, which is 0.6. Here are a few other equivalents to clarify this relationship:

% Transmittance	Opacity	Density
100	1	0
75	1.33	0.125
50	2	0.3
33.3	3	0.47
20	5	0.7
10	10	1.0
5	20	1.3
2	50	1.7
1	100	2.0

The Anatomy of a Film Curve

Now let's examine a film curve. Although these curves contain all the information needed to understand how the film will react to exposure and development, we'll start simply. The single curve shown here is a typical example (Fig. 3-2). Notice the calibration. The x-axis is calibrated in log E mcs units which increase from left to right, even though the numbers appear to increase from right to left. Remember that the numbers are *negative* logs and therefore stand for fractional values. The number $\overline{3}.0$ indicates 1/1000 mcs, the number $\overline{2}.0$ indicates 1/100 mcs, and $\overline{1}.0$ indicates 1/10 mcs. Experienced sensitometrists recognize immediately from these values that this is a moderately fast film because it is responding usefully to small amounts of exposure.

The y-axis of the graph is labelled "Density," which means that the numbers are logs and the values increase from bottom to top. Although

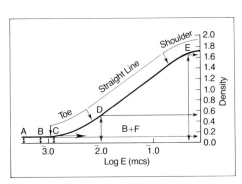

Figure 3-2. *A typical film curve.*

this axis is calibrated in increments of 0.2, the *scale* of calibration is the same as the scale of the exposure axis.

There are five points marked on the curve, each corresponding to a specific value of exposure, as indicated on the x-axis. Point A represents an exposure of much less than $\overline{3}.0$ and (projected across to the y-axis) a density of about 0.1. Point B indicates an exposure value considerably greater than A, but its density value is the same—about 0.1. This is significant; it shows that any exposure less than B will not be sufficient to affect the film at all. The 0.1 density recorded for both A and B is due to the film base material itself and to various influences which contribute to the faint cloudiness of the gelatin coating. It is called the *base-plus-fog* (B + F) density and is not useful image density.

Point C represents the threshold of sensitivity—the first indication that the film is responding to exposure by producing useful image density, distinguishable from base-plus-fog. Exposures greater than this, within reason, will affect the film usefully.

Point D appears in the *straight-line portion* of the characteristic curve, well within the film's useful range. Its exposure value of about $\overline{2}.0$ has produced a density in the negative of about 0.52. Point E lies on the drooping *shoulder* of the curve. Film exposure in this region is approaching saturation and the emulsion's ability to respond is decreasing. Image density at point E is excessively heavy because of the overexposure, and therefore this is not a desirable region to work in.

As you can see, the shape of the curve itself is an excellent indicator of the film's response to exposures of different values. In the region of "no response" the "curve" is a straight horizontal line, indicating no change in density for any change in exposure. The *toe* region marks the lower limit of useful exposure and is characterized by its upward curve or increasing *gradient*. In the toe region uniform increases of exposure result in an accelerated rate of increase in density.

Throughout the straight-line portion of the film curve, increases in exposure are responsible for proportionate increases in density. This doesn't mean, necessarily, that the increases are identical; doubling the exposure may increase density by only, say, 60%, but the *rate of change* is constant. Every time the exposure is increased the density will increase *proportionately*.

In the shoulder region exposure increases are accompanied by a decreasing rate of change in density until, when all the sensitive emulsion material has been thoroughly exposed, the curve levels out and indicates no further increase. Increasing the exposure beyond this point will eventually effectively desensitize the emulsion and result in *solarization*—an actual *decrease* in density as exposure increases. Except for special materials and special applications the curve shoulder and its region of solarization are never used on purpose, though we sometimes blunder in there by mistake.

Because both exposure and development are required to produce an image, supplying one without the other will leave the film without any trace of useful image. This is illustrated in Figure 3-3. The exposures of the film have not fallen within the film's useful range of sensitivity—in other words, the film hasn't been effectively exposed.

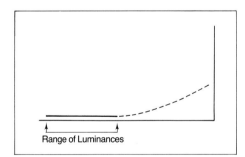

Figure 3-3. The film requires a certain amount of exposure effect (light intensity and time) to form a satisfactory image. Think of the various subject luminances as freight cars on a railroad track, moving from left to right along the exposure axis as film exposure increases. As the exposure builds up sufficiently to affect the film the luminance values slide up the film curves like a train turning onto a siding. There are any number of possible curves, each corresponding to a specific developing time.

Development has no effect on the unexposed film and the result is a clear "negative" whose only density is a uniform B + F density of about 0.1. The dotted extension of the curve illustrates the effect development would have had if the exposure had been adequate.

A fully exposed—but not developed—film will also produce a clear "negative" after fixation. Its curve will be similar; a straight horizontal line at about the 0.1 density level.

So far we've considered film curves exclusively, but paper curves are equally important. Both film and paper curves display the relationship between exposure (on the x-axis) and density (on the y-axis), but there are several differences between them. The most important one relates to the effect of development on image contrast. Most films gain in contrast as development is prolonged, as evidenced by the increasing gradient of the film curves (Fig. 3-4). Most papers, on the other hand, tend to reach maximum density and contrast quite quickly—typically in only a minute or so in the developer—and prolonging development *time* doesn't affect either the shape of the curve or its gradient very much (Fig. 3-5). Even with maximum development, most film curves won't exceed a gradient of more than 45° or so. Most papers, by comparison, display steep gradients, indicating relatively high contrast.

We'll investigate the characteristics of both films and papers at length in the following chapters. They're both important, but because the paper curves are relatively simple to comprehend, we'll begin our analysis there.

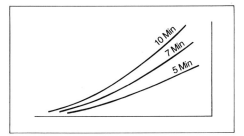

Figure 3-4. *Three typical film curves, each representing a particular time of development. The curve slope, or gradient, increases as development increases.*

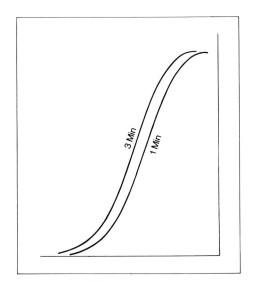

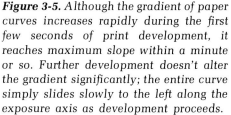

Figure 3-5. *Although the gradient of paper curves increases rapidly during the first few seconds of print development, it reaches maximum slope within a minute or so. Further development doesn't alter the gradient significantly; the entire curve simply slides slowly to the left along the exposure axis as development proceeds.*

David Bartlett

What the Curves Can Tell You

Paper characteristics are not as reliable and consistent as film characteristics. You're likely to find a noticeable variation in speed and contrast, or both, from one box of paper to the next, even boxes from the same emulsion batch. Also, it's not uncommon to find that two or three of the numbered contrast grades of some paper type are really quite similar in contrast, varying mainly in effective printing speed. Age and storage conditions affect speed and contrast; so can some development conditions, even though papers are usually developed to "completion."

Despite all these potential causes for error, it's possible to learn a lot by matching film and paper characteristics and the most efficient way to do this is to work with curves. Paper curves are hard to come by, however, because the major manufacturers don't publish them for specific paper types. They're not easy to plot yourself, either, unless you have a reflection densitometer or a suitably modified meter, as described in the Workbook. It is possible to gain an understanding of the working procedures, though, by practicing with typical curves (see the Workbook).

The Paper Curve

Because we're still talking about principles, we'll use a hypothetical paper curve (Fig. 4-1). As mentioned before, there are obvious differences between this curve and the film curves with which you are beginning to be familiar. First, the curve is much steeper, suggesting that it's a contrasty material. This high-contrast characteristic complements the typically low-contrast image formed by the film. Although this may sound haphazard and inefficient, it's not a bad system. If a negative were developed sufficiently to duplicate subject contrast, it would be excessively grainy and highlight definition would be de-

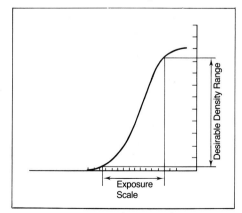

Figure 4-1. *A typical paper characteristic curve.*

graded. Thin, low-contrast negatives give the best image texture and sharpness, and are most satisfactory if they aren't *too* thin and flat to retain image details and gradation. Paper contrast can be high without penalty because print image grain is much too fine to be visible and image sharpness is never noticeably limited by paper characteristics.

Notice the shape of the paper curve. It's much more S-shaped than typical film curves are, and that implies tonal distortion. As you'll soon see, the paper is responsible for most of the difficulties you'll have with image gradation, and unfortunately it's relatively uncontrollable. The problem is magnified by the fact that almost the whole curve must be used in printing. You can't have muddy highlights in the print, which means that you must use the curve toe almost to the base-plus-fog level. You must have convincing blacks, too, which means working very close to the curve shoulder.

Although rich black accents in the print image give it zest and sparkle, it's risky to "print down" for a maximum black. The curves will show you why. Dark tones fall on the upper end of the paper curve with maximum black occurring at the extreme end of the shoulder where the gradient has diminished to a horizontal line. If you plot the densities for uniformly increasing increments of exposure, starting from middle gray and progressing to maximum black, you'll see how drastically contrast is reduced in the very dark tones (Fig. 4-2). Add to this that the eye is not very sensitive to density differences in the dark tones and you have two excellent reasons for keeping the important image tones from straying too far onto the curve shoulder.

Papers don't react to development in the same way that films do. In general, papers are developed in much more vigorous developers and developing times are relatively short. The print image appears, typically, in 10 to 30 seconds after immersion and is completed when the accent blacks are fully formed (Fig. 4-3), in about 1 or 2 minutes in most standard developers. Extending print developing time beyond this point of "completion" is not necessary for fine print quality and will only increase the risk of chemical and safelight fog. As a rule, the gradient of paper curves can't be usefully modified by variations in developing time. *Local* print contrast may *appear* to increase with forced development but the paper curves show that the curve slope is not noticeably affected. The curves simply drift to the left as development is extended and the image tones slide up the curve and over the shoulder like floating corks on an ocean wave. A similar effect can usually be obtained by increasing the print exposure and developing normally.

Print development, therefore, should be considered a relatively inflexible operation, except for unusual purposes. It doesn't matter what procedure you choose to follow if you develop long enough to produce maximum black in areas of full exposure and don't overdevelop to the point of risking fog. Consistency is critical—establish a procedure and stick to it.

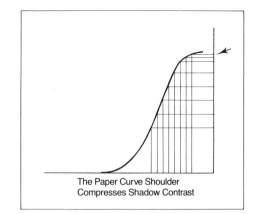

The Paper Curve Shoulder Compresses Shadow Contrast

Figure 4-2. *The vertical lines rising from the x-axis indicate uniformly increasing units of paper exposure. As they are reflected from the paper curve (representing development) they form horizontal lines which define units of increasing image density on the y-axis. Density and exposure increases are approximately proportional throughout the straight-line portion of the curve but the shoulder shortens the density units, indicating loss of shadow contrast.*

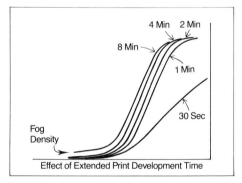

Effect of Extended Print Development Time

Figure 4-3. *Here is a typical paper curve family, showing the effect of increasing development. After maximum density is attained—typically in about 1 to 2 minutes—prolonging development merely moves the curves to the left without altering their shape or slope appreciably. Grossly extending the development time is likely to fog the highlights and may round off the shoulder contour slightly.*

Standards for Calibrating Paper Curves

Although paper characteristics are not as thoroughly described in the technical literature as film characteristics are, there are standards for establishing paper speed and useful exposure range. Figure 4-4 shows the ANSI method (American National Standard PH2.2-1966). The paper *speed point* is the exposure in mcs necessary to produce a print density of 0.6 over B + F and the useful density range (DR) is defined as running from a minimum density (Dmin) of 0.04 over base-plus-fog (paper white) to a maximum density (Dmax) of 90% of the maximum attainable density. The useful exposure range (ER) is found by dropping the Dmin and Dmax points down to the exposure axis. The ER is expressed in logs and is frequently referred to as the *Exposure Scale* or *ES*.

Print contrast is determined by paper and developer characteristics and is not much affected by variations in developing time. This print was exposed for 9 seconds and developed for 1 minute. Print 2 was exposed for 3 seconds and developed for 10 minutes. Except for slightly stained highlights and a minor difference in density, the 10-minute print is almost indistinguishable from the 1-minute print.

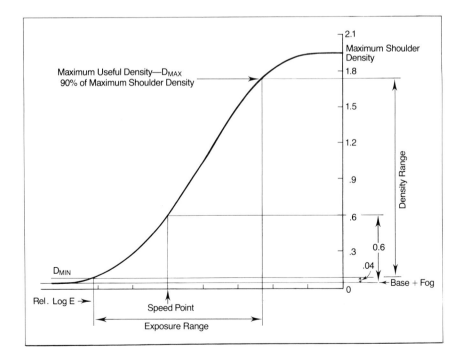

Figure 4-4. Here is a paper curve calibrated according to the recommendations of the American National Standards Institute (ANSI).

Exposure Scale vs. Density Range

Student photographers have trouble distinguishing between density range and exposure scale. *Density Range* refers to the range of print tones—blacks, grays, and whites—which results from exposure and development. All paper contrast grades of a particular brand, surface, and type have about the same density range; that is, they will all presumably produce about the same maximum density when properly exposed and developed. *Exposure Scale* refers to the range of exposing light intensities required to *produce* the density range. Exposure scale is different for each paper grade. A short ES implies a hard, contrasty paper; a long ES indicates a soft, low-contrast paper (Fig. 4-5).

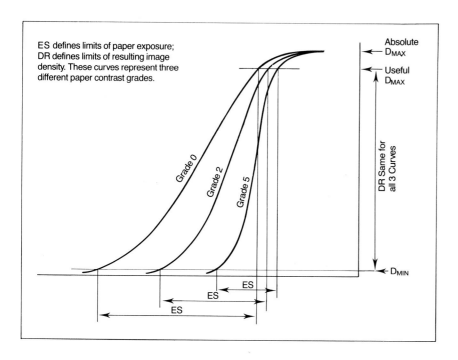

Figure 4-5. Different contrast grades of paper have different curves, as shown here. "Soft" papers—represented here by grade 0—require contrasty negatives, which is another way of saying they have long Exposure Scales. Normal papers work best with negatives of normal contrast—normal exposure scales—and "hard" papers require "flat" (low contrast) negatives because their exposure scales are short. All grades of the same brand, type, and surface are supposed to have similar density ranges, which means they should all produce about the same maximum density, but this is not always the case.

The Useful Limits of the Paper Curve

The print Dmax limit of 90% of maximum shoulder density, specified in the ANSI standard, may sound arbitrary, but tests have indicated that viewers prefer open, luminous shadows with good tonal separation to darker shadows in which details are obscured. If 2.0 represents the maximum shoulder density, it's advisable (in ANSI's opinion) to keep important image shadow details from exceeding a Dmax of about 1.8, for example. Although there is a visible difference between densities of 1.8 and 2.0, the difference is significant only when they are placed side by side for comparison. Without a darker tone for comparison, a Dmax of 1.8 will usually be satisfactory and will avoid the perils that lurk on the curve shoulder.

For your own purposes, of course, you can pick any Dmax you want and you'll probably find the ANSI specification very conservative—for some papers, at least. You don't have the same freedom of choice with the Dmin. Print whites darker than about 0.04 will look gray and dirty and a Dmin of much less than 0.04 risks loss of highlight separation, a result almost as disturbing as opaque shadows. The limits you select will determine the effective exposure scale of the paper—for you.

Since the negative densities are, in effect, the exposing lights for the paper, it would seem logical to assume that the negative DR and the paper ES should be the same. In some cases they are. If you make contact prints or if you use a diffusion enlarger, you can usually match the DR and ES without any problem. Condenser enlargers, however, tend to increase the effective negative contrast, so you'll probably find that you get best results by selecting a paper whose ES is somewhat greater than the negative DR (see appendix). Other enlarger types may require different compensations. "Point-source" condenser models may need a still larger ES, while dichroic color head enlargers, with their typical semi-diffused systems, may work best with some intermediate value of ES. In Chapter 9 we'll consider methods you can use to find appropriate values of DR and ES for your own purposes. When you've modified the ES value to fit your printing style, you can call it your "Scale Index"—a term frequently used to identify the working ES.

ASA scale on an exposure meter.

The Film Curves

When you press the shutter release on your camera, two factors—light intensity and time—will make up the effective film exposure. To be sure the exposure will be correct, though, you must first tell your meter how much light the film requires—by setting the ASA speed number into the calculator dial—and then measure the light at the subject to see what's available. The meter will show, by displaying appropriate pairs of apertures and shutter speeds, what proportion of the subject light must be admitted to the camera and for how long.

The film doesn't get just one exposure when you click the shutter. The subject reflects a wide range of light intensities or luminance values toward the lens and, although the *time* of exposure is uniform for all areas of the film, the light *intensity* is not. For this reason, some areas of the film are likely to be "underexposed" and some "overexposed," with subtle variations of exposure between these extremes.

Development of the latent image produces the visible image densities in approximate proportion to the exposure each area received. For this reason the negative highlights gain density much more rapidly than the shadow areas do, causing the characteristic curve slope—or gradient—to get progressively steeper as development proceeds (Fig. 4-6). The visible effect is one of increasing image contrast, which corresponds to a measurable increase in density range (Fig. 4-7).

It should now be apparent to you that a given subject luminance range, treated to some specific condition of development, will produce a specific negative density range. You should also recognize the three

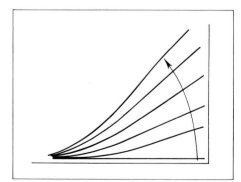

Figure 4-6. The film curve gradient increases as development proceeds.

33

possible variations of this relationship: if subject luminance range and curve gradient (G) are specified, negative density range can be determined (Fig. 4-8a); if SBR and DR are known, G can be found (Fig. 4-8b); and if G and DR are given, the SBR is easily discovered (Fig. 4-8c).

The range of light intensities that the subject reflects toward the camera is called the *subject luminance range*, but you'll frequently see it referred to as the *subject brightness range*. Technically, *luminance* is correct because it refers to measurable values of light produced by or reflected from the subject surfaces. The comparable term for measurable illumination in the subject area, before being reflected by the subject surfaces, is *illuminance*. *Brightness* properly refers to our *perception* of luminance or illuminance. It's like the difference between heat, which can be measured, and pain, which is our perception of heat. In spite of the fact that subject brightness range is incorrect, it is generally understood and its abbreviation, SBR, is distinctive and useful. ("SLR" can't be used because it means single-lens reflex, not subject luminance range, to most photographers.) You'll see both terms in this book but remember that SBR means subject luminance range.

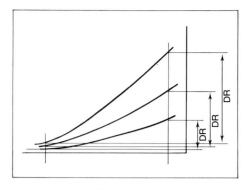

Figure 4-7. *As film development proceeds and gradient increases, the density range (DR) also increases.*

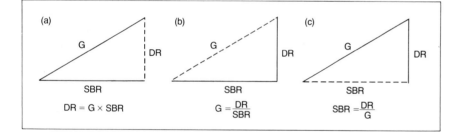

Figure 4-8. *The film curve "triangle" relationships: subject luminance range (SBR), curve slope or gradient (G), and density range (DR). Given G and SBR, find DR (a); given DR and SBR, find G (b); and given G and DR, find SBR (c).*

Curve Gradient Measurements: Gamma (γ)

Because the curve gradient is such an important characteristic, it must be defined precisely; there are several ways of doing so. If the gradient were a straight line, as in Figure 4-8a, b, and c, it would be possible to calibrate the slope in degrees; in practice, however, this is never done. Years ago the term *gamma* (γ) was frequently used to describe curve slope. The gamma number for any straight portion of the curve can be found by dividing the DR of the negative by the SBR (Fig. 4-9)—a procedure which you math wizards will recognize as the "tangent" function of angle a (Fig. 4-9). You can see that the gamma of any gradient less than 45° is going to be less than 1, which is another way of saying that the negative DR is less than the SBR. To phrase it a little differently, development to a gamma of less than 1 will *reduce* subject contrast, as it is recorded by the negative.

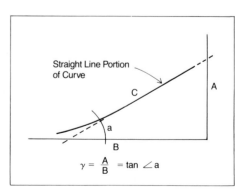

Figure 4-9. *Gamma (γ) relates only to the straight-line portion of the film curve.*

Gamma is not much used anymore because, by definition, it can only be computed on the straight-line portion of the film curve. This is awkward for two reasons. First, most modern film curves don't have much straight-line portion and, second, even if one is evident we're usually interested in including part of the curve toe region in our calculations. We still sometimes use the term loosely to refer to development contrast but most published data now define curve slope in terms of "average gradient" ($\overline{G}$) or, more frequently, in a special form of average gradient called Contrast Index (CI).

Average Gradient ($\overline{G}$). In the average gradient method, two points on the film curve are selected and connected with a straight line. When these points are projected down to the exposure axis, they define an SBR; when they are projected across to the density axis, they define a DR (Fig. 4-10). This forms a right triangle and the average gradient is found—just as gamma is—by dividing the DR by the SBR.

Ilford film curves are measured by the company's special version of the average gradient method (Fig. 4-11). The first point selected is at the 0.1-over-base-plus-fog level. Using this point as center, an arc of 1.5 radius (as measured along either axis) is drawn to intersect the upper section of the curve and define the second point. A straight line connecting the points represents the average gradient.

Contrast Index (CI). The Eastman Kodak Company uses a more complex $\overline{G}$ procedure and calls it *Contrast Index* (CI). To determine CI precisely you need a special protractor-like device to apply to the curve diagram; however, a good approximation of the CI values can be arrived at by following the Ilford procedure, using an arc radius of 2.0 rather than 1.5 (Fig. 4-12). Gamma, average gradient, and contrast index values for any given curve will probably be different because each deals with a different segment of the curve (Fig. 4-13). We'll generally use the generic term, average gradient ($\overline{G}$), because it can be considered to include both gamma and CI measurements. Also, $\overline{G}$ values are more useful for our purposes because they can be used to measure gradient over any selected section of the curve—which is desirable in working with a fixed value of density range. Contrast index values—although ingeniously derived—often don't measure the section of the curve we're interested in using. Like gamma measurements, they're useful laboratory standards but not very practical for personal calibration of materials.

Curve Gradient vs. Developing Time

Since gamma, average gradient, and contrast index numbers represent specific film and (especially) development conditions, they can be displayed in graph form, plotted against developing time—if such factors as developer temperature, agitation, and dilution are held constant. You've probably seen lots of these charts but, in case you're not familiar with them, Figure 4-14 is a typical one.

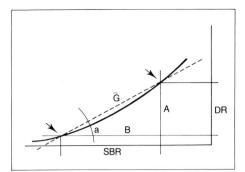

Figure 4-10. *Average Gradient ($\overline{G}$) defines the average slope between any two selected points on the film curve. The points are connected with a straight line which forms the hypotenuse of the standard film triangle; then,* $\overline{G} = \dfrac{DR}{SBR}$.

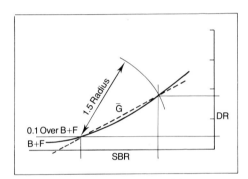

Figure 4-11. *The published $\overline{G}$ values for Ilford films are found by a special procedure, as shown here. From the 0.1-over-base-plus-fog point on the curve, an arc of 1.5 radius is drawn, intersecting the curve to find the second point. When these points are connected with a straight line the standard film triangle is formed and* $\overline{G} = \dfrac{DR}{SBR}$.

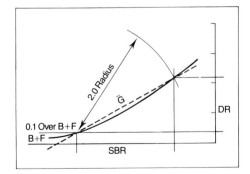

Figure 4-12. *Kodak's Contrast Index (CI) values can be approximated by following Ilford's method, but using a radius of 2.0. Then,* $CI\ (approximately) = \dfrac{DR}{SBR}$.

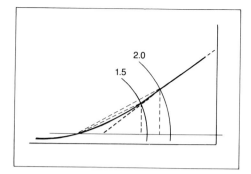

Figure 4-13. *The three methods of measuring curve slope, compared: On this hypothetical film curve,*
$$Gamma = 0.73$$
$$Ilford's \ \overline{G} = 0.52$$
$$Kodak's \ CI = 0.55$$

Presumably, if you develop to a particular $\overline{G}$ number, regardless of the film or developer used, all your well-exposed negatives of any given SBR should exhibit the same contrast and print on the same paper grade. The numbers can help you match abnormal subject ranges to "normal" paper, too. For example, if you encounter a subject whose luminance range is 8 stops, or 2.4, and you want to produce a negative with a DR of 1.1, you can determine the necessary $\overline{G}$ number by dividing 1.1 by 2.4:

$$\overline{G} = \frac{DR}{SBR} \ \text{or} \ \frac{1.1}{2.4} = 0.458 \ \text{or about} \ .46$$

Look up the developing time for a $\overline{G}$ of 0.46 on the chart and develop accordingly. In later chapters you'll learn to derive your own working charts from characteristic curves you've plotted yourself.

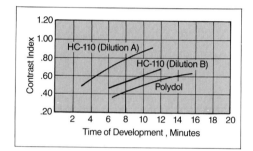

Figure 4-14. *A typical "time vs. CI" chart.*
© Eastman Kodak Company, 1976

Film and Paper Speeds

You've seen how characteristic curves can be made to yield development information; they can also supply information about the effective speed or sensitivity of films and papers. If you prepare a graph with a very long exposure axis and plot on it the curve families of several different films and papers, you'll see that the faster materials are located near the left of the graph axis, where the exposures are minimal, and the slower materials' curves appear toward the right, in the region of relatively great exposure.

For example (Fig. 4-15), if you plot the curve families for Royal Pan, Commercial sheet film, and Kodak Polycontrast printing paper on the same graph, the exposure axis will extend from about $\overline{3}.0$ mcs to about 2.5 mcs. The Royal Pan curves will start at about $\overline{3}.0$ and extend to the right, overlapping the several curves which make up the Commercial family, which will begin at about $\overline{1}.0$. The Commercial curves, in turn, will overlap the Polycontrast family, which will occupy an area from about 0.8 to about 2.3, or so. If you want to include Azo—Kodak's lovely contact printing paper—you'll have to extend the calibration to

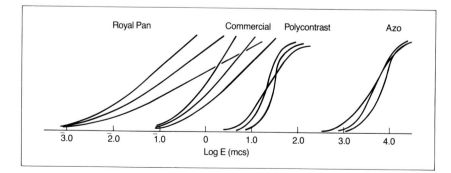

Figure 4-15. *Comparison of the approximate relative speeds of various sensitized materials.*

36

about 4.0. This is a graphic way of saying that Royal Pan is something like a million times faster than Azo, an interesting, if not very useful, statistic.

The speed of a film or paper establishes the *position* of its characteristic curve family on the exposure axis (Fig. 4-16). During the film exposure, the subject luminances arrange themselves along the graph exposure axis—shadow luminances on the left and highlight luminances toward the right—and the whole line (the SBR) slides along the x-axis from left to right as the exposure increases. This is illustrated in Figure 4-17. In each case. the film speed (curve placement), developing time (curve slope), and SBR (length of the subject luminance line) are constant and only the camera exposure varies. Curve *a* shows the effect of underexposure, which leaves a portion of the SBR outside the useful region of the film curve, as indicated by the Dmin (minimum density) and Dmax (maximum density) lines.

When the SBR is projected up to the curve and across to the density axis, it is apparent that two units of subject shadow detail will not appear on the negative as useful densities. Curve *b* shows a normal exposure. In this case the SBR values, projected up to the film curve, fill the entire space between Dmin and Dmax and the resulting negative contains a useful record of all the subject values. Curve *c* illustrates overexposure. The SBR values, projected vertically to the curve, begin at about mid-curve and run beyond the desired Dmax. This negative contains a record of all the subject values but all densities are excessively heavy.

From these illustrations, it should be clear that for any given condition of development "perfect" exposure will place the subject values directly under the film curve so that the darkest value, projected vertically, falls just inside the ideal Dmin limit and the lightest highlight just reaches the ideal Dmax limit. Any other exposure will cause the negative either to lose some desirable shadow detail or to become unnecessarily dense.

How Development Affects Film Speed

Perfect exposure alone is not sufficient to guarantee ideal placement of the SBR values on the film curve. As Figure 4-18 shows, three films given identical "normal" exposure, but developed for different lengths of time, will produce three quite different negatives. Curve *a*, representing underdevelopment, yields a negative which has perilously thin shadow density and short density range. Curve *b* describes a normal negative, and curve *c* shows the heavy negative density and high contrast—long DR—that result from overdevelopment. In these curves it's apparent that underdevelopment produces less shadow density and overdevelopment builds up more density than is desirable. These density problems can be corrected by changing the film exposure (Fig. 4-19). Here, underdevelopment (curve *a*) has been counteracted by increased exposure, as indicated by the shift of the SBR to the right along the exposure axis. The normal negative (curve *b*) is unchanged.

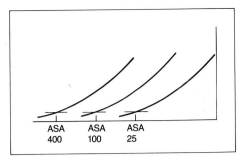

Figure 4-16. *Film speed establishes the position of the curve along the exposure axis.*

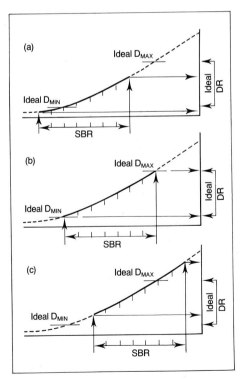

Figure 4-17. *Increasing camera exposure slides all the subject tones to the right along the exposure axis.*

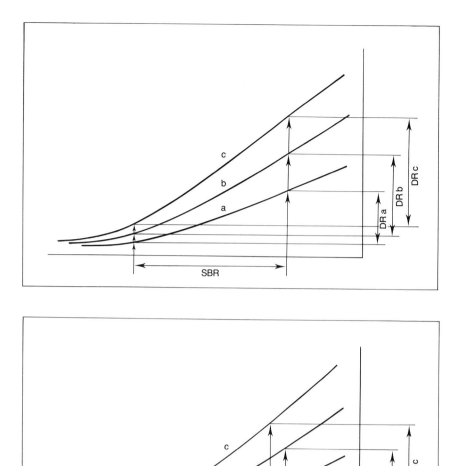

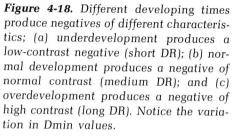

Figure 4-18. Different developing times produce negatives of different characteristics; (a) underdevelopment produces a low-contrast negative (short DR); (b) normal development produces a negative of normal contrast (medium DR); and (c) overdevelopment produces a negative of high contrast (long DR). Notice the variation in Dmin values.

Figure 4-19. Dmin variations can be reduced by adjusting film exposure to match developing time: (a) overexposure compensates for underdevelopment; (b) normal condition, unchanged; (c) underexposure compensates for overdevelopment. Notice: these corrections apply to Dmin only; in this illustration negative DR is not significantly affected by changes in film exposure.

The heavy Dmin, typical of overdevelopment (curve c), has been prevented by underexposing the film slightly to shift its SBR to the left.

Mid-tone and highlight densities are not particularly critical, within reasonable limits, but shadow densities must be well-formed. The Dmin point on the film curve is selected with this in mind. No image details should fall below Dmin if you want to preserve luminous, open shadow detail in the final print. Because shadow exposure is so critical, Dmin becomes the logical calibration point for establishing film speed. In your own work you can adopt any Dmin you like. As you will see in subsequent chapters, it isn't even necessary to be consistent about it. Sometimes it's advantageous to shoot for a higher-than-normal Dmin (when shadow detail must be emphasized, for example) and sometimes it's desirable to use a lower-than-normal one. However, when you change your Dmin from the accepted "normal," remember that you're changing the effective speed of your film.

Actually, you don't need to be concerned about this. The familiar published film speeds are only suggestions, not laws. If you are print-quality-conscious—and especially if you use sheet film—you've probably already made some adjustment in the published speed of your film. Most likely you've de-rated it so that you'll "overexpose" a little. Quite a few photographers do this after discovering that the ASA speeds are a little too high for best results. This is true because they're based on an unrealistic "normal" condition of development. You must realize, of course, that not everyone agrees about what's "normal."

How Film Speeds Are Determined

Briefly, the ASA film speeds are derived from the exposure value required to produce a density of 0.1-over-base-plus-fog when the film development is such that an SBR of 1.3 will produce a negative DR of 0.8. These specifications are demonstrated in Figure 4-20. The Dmin of 0.1 is called the *speed point* and that exposure in lux-seconds—divided into the constant 0.8—is translated into the speed number.

Although it isn't mentioned in the specifications, the ASA standard curve has a $\overline{G}$ value of about 0.62. We haven't discussed "normal" gradients yet, but a value of about 0.5 is probably more appropriate for most "normal" work than 0.62 is. You've already seen that reducing development will lower negative density, so it follows that exposing your film at its ASA rating and developing it for a $\overline{G}$ of less than 0.62 will give you thinner negatives than you'd like to work with. Several factors may influence the size of the error, but Figure 4-21 illustrates the principle. The ASA standard curve, labelled 0.62, is shown as part of a curve family and its official SBR of 1.3—13 exposure units of 0.1 each—is indicated in the proper position. The curve labelled 0.5 represents a more usual condition of development, obviously less than standard. The third curve illustrates an extreme overdevelopment condition, for purposes of comparison.

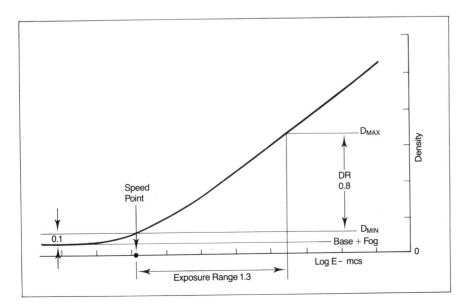

Figure 4-20. This is the way film speeds are determined, as stipulated by the American National Standards Institute (ANSI), originally the American Standards Association (ASA). This standard is now being superseded by an international standard, but these procedures are unchanged.

Effective Film Speed (EFS)

If we consider Dmin's of 0.1 over base-plus-fog to be desirable in all three negatives, they can be called the "speed points" of the individual curves. Projecting these speed points down to the exposure axis indicates the exposure value required to produce each, and a comparison of these exposure values provides us with relative speed ratings for the three development conditions. Assuming that the assigned ASA speed of this film is 125, we'll mark that speed at the speed point of the standard curve. Notice that the speed point for curve *a* is almost one exposure unit to the left of the ASA normal speed point, indicating that less exposure is required. The *c* curve speed point, on the other hand, falls about two units to the right, indicating a need for more than "normal" exposure. Now, since a need for less exposure is equivalent to an increase in effective film speed and a need for more exposure indicates an effective speed loss, we can calibrate the curves. Each exposure unit equals ⅓ stop, equivalent to a log unit of 0.1, which is the interval between the numbers in the standard ASA sequence of film speeds. Therefore, curve *a*, which is 0.1 faster than the normal 125, is effectively 160, whereas curve *c*—0.2 slower than 125—is effectively only 80. In this hypothetical case, setting the ASA speed of 125 into your meter and developing for a realistic $\overline{G}$ of 0.5 will result in an underexposure of ⅔ stop.

In summary, negative density and contrast can be controlled by varying film exposure and development. Print density can be controlled by variations in paper exposure and, to some extent, development. Print contrast is essentially determined by the inherent contrast characteristic of the paper itself, and is not much affected by changes in developing time. In putting these controls to practical use, the subject luminance range dictates film developing time, which in turn determines effective film speed. Much of the rest of this book is devoted to consideration of the implications and ramifications of this simple concept.

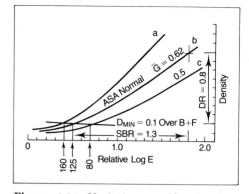

Figure 4-21. *Variations in film development alter the effective film speed.*

The Tone Reproduction Cycle

Now we can trace the subject values through film and paper curves to the final print image. Let's assume that we're using a diffusion enlarger so the negative DR and the paper ES can be the same. We'll also assume an SBR of 7 stops, or 2.1. Figure 4-22 shows how the

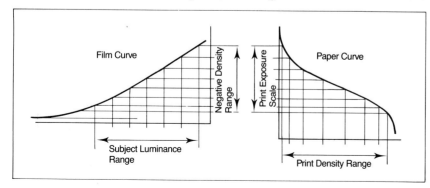

Figure 4-22. *Subject tonal relationships (gradation) are distorted as they are translated to form the print image. Here the seven equal divisions of the subject luminance range result in seven unequal divisions of print density.*

subject values are translated into negative densities and demonstrates how they are distorted in the process. The negative densities are arranged along the paper exposure axis to provide the print exposure. The paper curve carries the tone distortion still further. The magnitude of the process distortion becomes obvious when the print values are compared with those of the original subject (Fig. 4-23).

As a further illustration of the critical nature of the printing process in the reproduction of tone, Figure 4-24 shows the effect of a half-stop increase in print exposure. Extending print developing time substantially will have approximately the same effect on the image tones. You can see the relatively minor difference in extreme highlight and shadow rendering compared with the obvious shift in mid-tone values (Fig. 4-25). As mentioned previously, this effect is sometimes misinterpreted as being an effective increase in paper contrast grade when print development is extended.

You should now have a good understanding of characteristic curves. You should comprehend the relationships between subject luminance range, film developing time, film exposure, and paper grade. You should also be more aware of the tone distortion inherent in the process and begin to appreciate the subtle adjustments of gradation which are possible.

Now let's go on to practical problems. In the next chapters we'll distill working information from the curves and proceed through a general discussion of exposure-development control systems to the famous Zone System—and beyond.

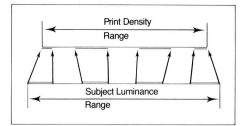

Figure 4-23. *Subject luminance values and print densities compared.*

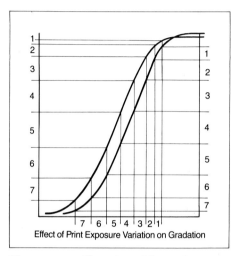

Figure 4-24. *Changing either print exposure or development will affect print density and gradation similarly, but with no significant effect on the curve shape or gradient.*

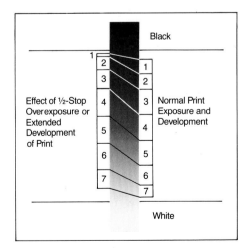

Figure 4-25. *This shows how print values are shifted by increases in either exposure or development.*

CHAPTER
5

From Theory
to Practice

Although the photographic image can be modified at every stage of the process, control is greatest during film exposure and development. Usually, you can't manipulate the subject itself—except, of course, when you are working in the studio. The printing process is only slightly more flexible. Image contrast and density can be altered by changes in paper grade and exposure, and local modifications can be made by dodging or burning in, but print controls should be used with discretion. Think of them as techniques for refining the image characteristics rather than drastically altering them.

Any type and contrast grade of paper will yield best results with negatives of a specific density range. This means that you're faced with the problem of having to produce negatives of nearly identical DR from subjects that may vary widely in luminance range. As you learned in the previous chapter, you can do this in all but the most extreme situations by adjusting film exposure and development to compensate for variations in SBR.

You now know that the effective speed of the film is related to development. You also know that development is determined by SBR. It follows, therefore, that SBR influences effective film speed. These are vital bits of information that can be extracted easily from the film curves and condensed into chart form for practical use. You are already familiar with the general procedures for doing this so let's apply them to a real curve family—Tri-X sheet film, tray-developed with constant agitation in D-76, diluted 1:1, at 20°C (68°F) (Fig. 5-1). In the following instructions, each step is illustrated separately. Then a complete curve family is shown with all the construction lines in place, as they would appear in actual use. I recommend that you use the worksheet (page 39 in the Workbook) to complete your own curve analysis, following the instructions below.

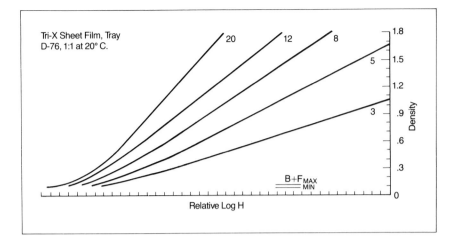

Figure 5-1. Characteristic curve family; Tri-X sheet film, developed in a tray with constant agitation in D-76, diluted 1:1, at 20°C.

Drawing Tools and Tips

The construction involves some simple mechanical drawing. If you have never done it before, a few suggestions may be in order. You'll need a few basic tools: a small drawing board, a small T square, an 8-inch or 10-inch 60°/30° triangle, a french curve, some compasses, a ruler, preferably one with metric scales as well as inches, drafting or masking tape, scissors, pencils, and an eraser. (All of these items can be purchased at your local art supply store.)

When you've assembled your drawing tools, position the worksheet on the drawing board so that the horizontal lines on the worksheet are parallel to the T square. Then tape the upper corners of the sheet to the drawing board.

The T square is used as a guide for drawing all horizontal lines. Be sure the "T" of the T square is pressed firmly against the edge of the drawing board so that the lines will be straight and parallel to each other. Vertical lines are drawn using the triangle and T square in combination. First, position the T square a little below the space where the vertical line will be drawn, then slide the triangle along it into position. Hold both T square and triangle firmly in place as you draw the line. It's best to hold the pencil nearly vertical, angled slightly so that the point of the pencil touches the guiding edge. Always draw the first construction lines lightly so they can be erased if necessary, then strengthen the essential ones later.

The triangle and T square are also used to draw 30° and 60° angles but you'll rarely need these. Other diagonal lines are drawn using the triangle, or other straightedge, without the T square. Hold the triangle firmly in the desired position and draw as usual. The same technique is used with the french curve. First indicate the general direction and shape of the desired curved line with dots or lightly sketched lines. Then find the appropriate edge of the french curve, position it to follow the guide points as closely as possible, and trace it as far as is suitable with the pencil (Fig. 5-2). You may have to position the french curve several times to complete the drawing. Try to connect the separate line segments neatly so the finished curve will be smooth and flowing.

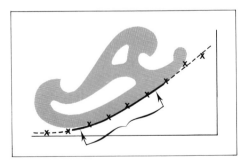

Figure 5-2. Follow the edge of the french curve only as far as it coincides with the data points and the sketched curve line. Then reposition it and draw another line segment. Continue this procedure until the line is complete.

44

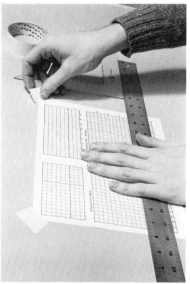

Align the horizontal lines of the worksheet with the T square, then tape the upper corners of the worksheet to the drawing board.

The T square is used as a guide for drawing horizontal lines. Be sure the "T" of the T square is pressed firmly against the edge of the drawing board.

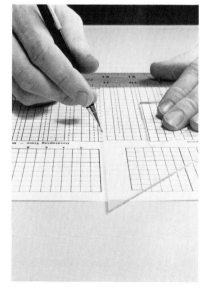

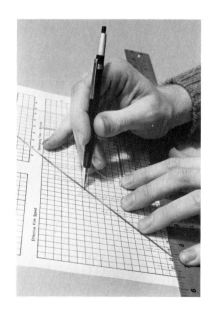

The triangle is used for drawing vertical and diagonal lines.

45

Curve Analysis

Locating Dmin. To begin the curve analysis, locate the Dmin points on the curve toes. Although this can be done most accurately by measuring the values separately for each curve in the family, it is usually satisfactory to locate the points on the first and last curve and connect them with a straight line. This has been done in Figure 5-3, using a Dmin value of 0.1-over-base-plus-fog. It's safe to assume that the Dmin line defines a useful minimum density on each of the curves it crosses as well as on any new curve which may be drawn into the family later on.

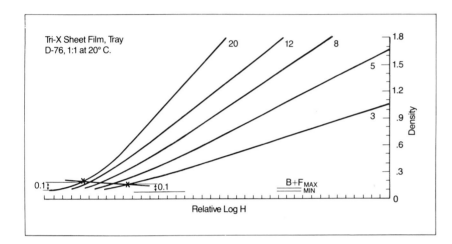

Figure 5-3. Locate on the first and last curves the point on each that represents a density of 0.1-over-base-plus-fog. Connect these two points with a straight line to establish Dmin for the curve family.

Locating Dmax. Now the Dmax points on each of the curves can be found. This has been done in Figure 5-4, using a DR of 1.0, for the purpose of illustration. Measure vertically from each Dmin point a distance equivalent to a log interval of 1.0, and project each point across to its appropriate curve to locate Dmax. Then connect the Dmax points with a ruled line. Again, for practical purposes, you can locate the points on the first and last curves and connect them to find the Dmax limits on the intervening curves. The vertical distance between Dmin and Dmax on each curve should now be 1.0—the selected DR.

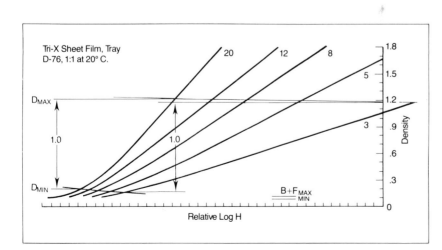

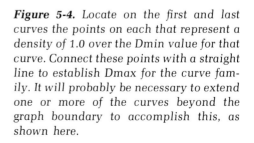

Figure 5-4. Locate on the first and last curves the points on each that represent a density of 1.0 over the Dmin value for that curve. Connect these points with a straight line to establish Dmax for the curve family. It will probably be necessary to extend one or more of the curves beyond the graph boundary to accomplish this, as shown here.

Determining the SBR. The Dmin and Dmax points define the useful density limits of the film curves. In other words, negative densities greater than Dmax or less than Dmin will not be recorded as useful shadow or highlight detail in the print. Similarly, the Dmax and Dmin points, projected down to the exposure axis, define the useful limits of the SBR. No subject luminance value which falls to the left of the Dmin point or to the right of the Dmax point will be detailed satisfactorily in the print. Find the SBR for each curve by measuring the horizontal distance between its Dmax and Dmin, as illustrated in Figure 5-5. Then label each curve with its SBR in stops, as shown. Since each curve results from a specific developing time, it's now possible to plot the SBR-vs.-developing-time chart. Complete your own chart on a worksheet, page 51 of the Workbook, using the data from your drawing.

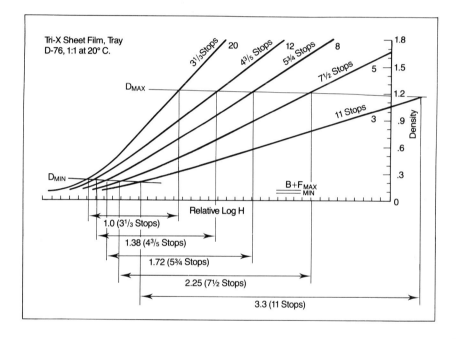

Figure 5-5. Drop vertical lines from the Dmin and Dmax points on each curve and measure the horizontal distance between the lines to find the SBR for each curve in log numbers. Convert these SBR values to stops (by dividing by 0.3) and use them to label each curve.

Finding Effective Film Speeds

Film speed calculation is a little more complicated, but not difficult once you get the idea. It is based on the ASA standard method and involves constructing a new curve in the existing family. This new curve must satisfy the ASA specifications, namely a Dmin of 0.1-over-base-plus-fog, an SBR of 1.3, and a DR of 0.8. It's easy to locate the new curve if you construct the ASA triangle on a piece of paper, using the same scale that is used in constructing the film curve graph.

For the practice drawing, use the triangle on page 55 of the Workbook. Cut the triangle out carefully and position it in the curve family so the triangle base is parallel to the graph exposure axis and the lower vertex of the triangle touches the Dmin line. Now slide the triangle along the Dmin line until the vertices of its acute angles fall between the same pair of the film curves and are spaced between the curves in proportionate positions. In other words, if the lower vertex falls halfway between curves 2 and 3, the upper vertex must also fall halfway between curves 2 and 3. If the lower vertex is 4/5 of the way between curves 3 and 4 at the 0.1-over-base-plus-fog density level, the upper vertex must similarly be placed 4/5 of the way between curves 3 and 4, at *its* density level.

Figure 5-6 shows the triangle improperly positioned in the curve family. In *a* the triangle vertices don't fall between the same pair of curves. In *b* the vertices are between the same pair of curves but not proportionately spaced between them. In *c* the triangle satisfies all the requirements except one: its lower vertex is not on the Dmin line. In *d* the vertices appear to be spaced properly but the base is not parallel to the horizontal axis of the graph. Figure 5-7 shows the triangle properly positioned; this is its only possible location in the curve family.

When the triangle is correctly placed, its point of contact with the Dmin line corresponds to the speed point from which the published ASA speed of the film was derived. Although it's unlikely that this point is absolutely accurate, it serves as a convenient reference point for assigning relative speeds to the various curves. In most cases the error is negligible, but if a significant error does exist it can be corrected easily during the initial field tests.

Assigning effective speeds to the various curves is now simple. Project the "official" speed point down to the exposure axis and label it

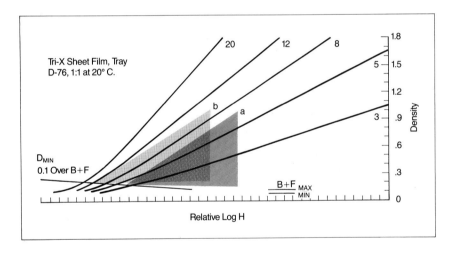

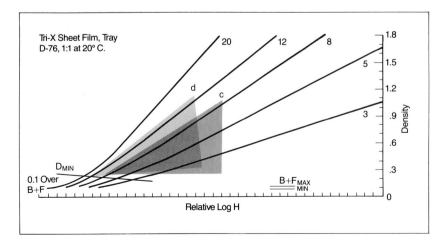

Figure 5-6. In determining the effective film speed with the "ASA triangle" the position of the triangle in the curve family is critical. Here are four errors to avoid. In (a) the triangle vertices don't fall between the same pair of film curves. In (b) the vertices fall between the same pair of curves but not in the same relative position between them. In (c) the triangle doesn't touch the Dmin line. In (d) its base is not parallel to the x-axis of the graph.

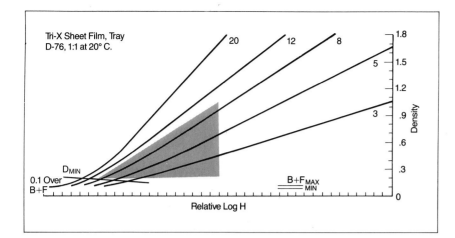

Figure 5-7. Here the ASA triangle is shown properly positioned in the film curve family. No other placement can satisfy all the requirements.

"ASA normal" or—in this case—"ASA 320" because that's the published speed of Tri-X sheet film. Then project the other Dmin points down to the exposure axis to find their positions relative to the ASA point (Fig. 5-8). Remember, consecutive numbers in the ASA film speed series represent speed point shifts of 0.1 in log units and the film speed numbers decrease to the right and increase to the left along the exposure axis.

It will be easy to calibrate the various speed points if you prepare a little film speed ruler, marked in intervals of 0.1 and labelled with ASA numbers, as shown in Figure 5-9 and printed on page 55 of the Workbook. Be sure the ruler calibrations are in the same scale as the graph. Cut the ruler out and place it below and parallel to the exposure axis so that the appropriate film speed number—320 in this case—is aligned with the "ASA normal" line. Then read the other speeds as accurately as possible. Since it's unlikely that the speed points will fall exactly on the ruler numbers, you'll have to interpolate a little. Use plusses and minuses to qualify the numbers. For example, if a point falls less than halfway between 250 to 320, call it "250+." If a point is closer to 160 than 125, call it "160−." Then label each of the curves with its effective speed number as illustrated in Figure 5-8, and plot the effective-film-speed-vs.-SBR chart on page 51 of the Workbook.

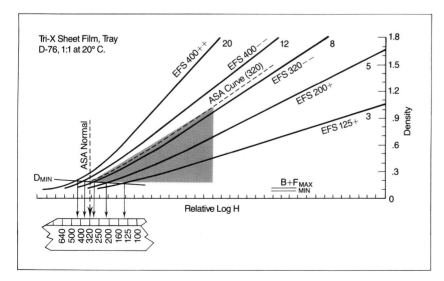

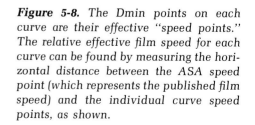

Figure 5-8. The Dmin points on each curve are their effective "speed points." The relative effective film speed for each curve can be found by measuring the horizontal distance between the ASA speed point (which represents the published film speed) and the individual curve speed points, as shown.

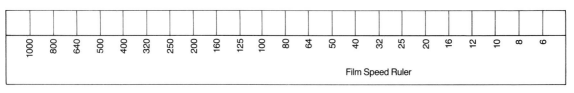

Figure 5-9. *A film speed ruler makes effective film speed determination easy. Be sure the ruler is in the same scale as the film curve graph; each division of the film speed ruler must equal a log interval of 0.1 on the graph axes.*

The Completed Construction

Figure 5-10 shows the film curve family with all the construction lines in place. If you have followed the instructions and completed the worksheet drawing, compare it with this illustration. Check your working charts against Figures 5-11 and 5-12, and review the instructions if you find any significant errors.

This Tri-X curve family—and the other curve families we'll cover in this book—are based on actual tests which provided useful working data for the persons who constructed them. They may or may not prove reliable for you, as given. If not, there are several reasons why: the film itself may have been changed or superseded, your thermometer may not agree with the one used in the test, your tap water may affect developer activity, your agitation procedures are probably different from those used in the test, or your film may have been more or less affected by age and storage conditions.

In spite of these potential problems the information is worth trying. It is based on using Kodak Polycontrast paper, with a #2 filter, exposed under a condenser enlarger. If you print with a diffusion enlarger (which will tend to produce lower image contrast) you should modify the data. Using another worksheet, redraw the construction lines with a negative DR of about 1.2 instead of 1.0. If you prefer to use some other paper, select the appropriate ES value from the chart in the

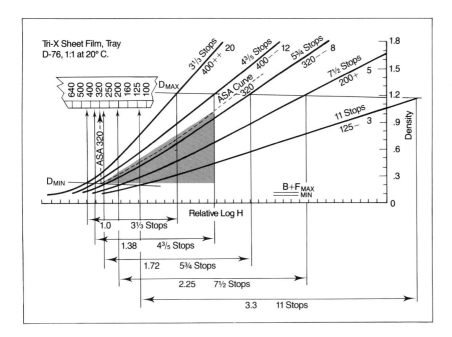

Figure 5-10. *Here is the curve family with all construction lines shown and the curves labelled with the pertinent working information: SBR in stops, EFS numbers, and developing times.*

appendix, page 175. Changing the DR will alter both working charts because it will change the SBRs.

You now have the technical information necessary to control the photographic process from subject to print (using Tri-X, D-76 1:1, and Polycontrast), condensed into handy chart form. Although conventional metering procedures will not permit you to take full advantage of this information, you'll find it well worth using.

Carry the effective-film-speed-vs.-SBR chart with you when you photograph and use it to determine the appropriate film speed setting for each subject condition you recognize. This setting—coupled with sensible metering procedures—should improve the accuracy and consistency of your exposures. Back in the darkroom, consult the developing-time-vs.-SBR chart and develop the film accordingly. In every case, exposure and development will be matched to provide negatives of consistent Dmin and DR—assuming, of course, that you've plotted your test curves accurately and used the data wisely. In the next few chapters I'll show you how to put these working charts to practical use.

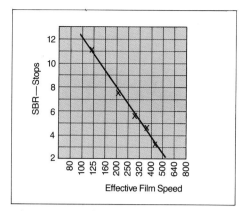

Figure 5-11. *Plotting the values of SBR against values of EFS for each curve produces this working chart which displays the appropriate film speed value for every condition of subject luminance range.*

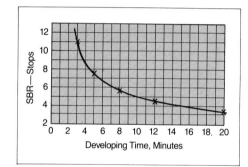

Figure 5-12. *Plotting SBR values against developing times gives you this working information: the appropriate developing time for any subject luminance range.*

CHAPTER
6

Putting Your Data to Work

Most authorities agree that a subject luminance range of 7 stops can be called "normal." Whether it really is normal is not important, but we do need a basis for calculation and this is as good as any other. We'll consider the 7 stops to include all the subject luminances that will appear in the print as detailed or textured tones, specifically excluding solid black and pure white. The darkest extreme of the 7-stop range will still be distinguishable from the accent blacks and the lightest white tone will have a barely discernible shade to differentiate it from pure paper white. Some authorities have included black and white in the "normal" range and called it 9 stops and some consider 10 stops normal, but we'll work with 7, not including the accents.

It would be convenient technically—but tiresome visually—if every subject exhibited this 7-stop range, featuring uniform and consistent gradation from dark to light. If this were the case, a general *reflectance* meter reading of the subject area would indicate an average luminance value which would be identical with the luminance of the subject mid-tone, or middle gray. In other words, the average reading would be 3½ stops higher than the luminance value of the deepest shadow, and 3½ stops lower than a reading taken from the lightest textured highlight. This is not usually the case. Most subjects do not contain equivalent areas of light and dark values, nor is their average luminance the same as their middle gray luminance.

What the Reflectance Meter Reads and What It Means

It makes no difference to a meter whether the subject consists of many dissimilar areas of tone, including some extremes, or whether it consists of a single, uniform tone. If the total light energy reaching its cell is the same, the meter will tell you the exposure should be the

Left: The well-known Surrealist painter and sculptor, Gerry Kamrowski, at home. If all the tones in this subject area were averaged they'd approximate a middle gray. A reflectance meter can't distinguish between a subject of this sort and a uniform area of similar average tone (above). Photograph by Tom Drew.

same. The meter, in other words, simply responds to light; it is not aware of subject matter nor does it have any idea what you intend to do with the information it provides. In this sense it's a *light meter*, not an *exposure meter*.

It becomes an exposure meter as soon as you transfer its light reading onto its calculating scale. There, the measurement of light intensity is weighed against the sensitivity of the film, as indicated by its ASA rating, and the camera settings are displayed. It is very important to keep in mind that these settings are pertinent only for use with a normal 7-stop-range subject whose average luminance is equivalent to middle gray.

The meter is programmed to treat every subject as if it were normal and "assumes" you want every subject area you point it at to turn into a middle gray value in the print. Therefore, if you use it as an *exposure meter*, and point it at a white object, it will give you exposure information that will turn that object gray in the print. Point it at a gray object, you'll get a gray image; point it at a black object, you'll get a gray image, and so on.

If the meter could be trained to read a white object and provide information that would produce a white image, or look at black and produce a black image, a useful camera setting could be based on any reading. All the meter can do, however, is supply accurate information for gray objects—or average luminances which equal gray—and the decision-making is up to you. There are several ways to deal with this. One approach is to let the meter have its way: if it can deal effectively only with gray, give it gray to read!

The Gray Card

There are standard gray cards of 18% reflectance (equivalent to a reflection density of about 0.75) available for this purpose. Place one of these in the subject position and take the meter reading of the gray surface, being sure the card is illuminated just as the subject is. Then place the meter light reading opposite the normal pointer on the calculating dial; the indicated camera settings should be suitable for recording the full range of shadows, middle tones, and highlight details of a normal subject—assuming, of course, that the film is developed normally.

The gray card meter reading is correct only for the value of gray represented by the card itself. That is, the gray card luminance is the only value the meter will succeed in rendering as a middle gray in the print. From the meter's point of view, subject luminances lighter than the gray card will be "overexposed" and will print as light tones. Similarly, subject luminances darker than middle gray will be "underexposed" and will appear in the print as darker than the gray card value. This, of course, is ideal because it means the subject tones will be recorded in the print the way the photographer visualized them. The meter, of course, would prefer to have everything gray; a uniform, unmodulated gray.

Reflectance meters measure average luminance; if the subject is uniformly middle gray, or made up of various areas of tone that average middle gray, the meter will consider the subject "normal" and suggest camera settings that can be used without compensation. Below left: Kearey Campbell meters a standard gray card to determine the exposure for a parking structure. Below right: The light gray concrete areas and the darker interior spaces of the parking structure average approximately middle gray so the meter reading from the gray card is applicable.

Taking the meter reading from the standard gray card avoids a few problems that averaging-type reflectance meters frequently encounter. One—already alluded to—will arise if the subject is predominantly light or dark in tone, that is, if its average reflectance reading is not equivalent to the luminance of a middle gray. If the average reflectance is lighter than middle gray the meter will advise you to underexpose; if darker, the meter will call for more exposure than desirable and the image will be overexposed.

The field of a typical hand-held reflectance meter—that is, the area it is actually measuring—is not clearly defined. If the subject contains areas of varied size and tone it is almost impossible to be sure you are

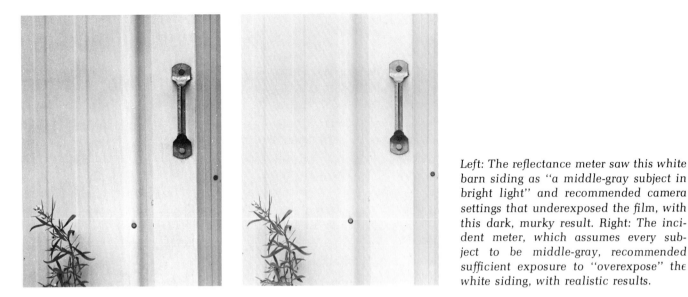

Left: The reflectance meter saw this white barn siding as "a middle-gray subject in bright light" and recommended camera settings that underexposed the film, with this dark, murky result. Right: The incident meter, which assumes every subject to be middle-gray, recommended sufficient exposure to "overexpose" the white siding, with realistic results.

pointing the meter at a "mix" of luminances that will equal the necessary middle gray average. This uncertainty is reduced with the built-in meters in single-lens-reflex cameras because their field of view usually coincides with the viewfinder image. The meter's field is usually "weighted," though, which means the meter doesn't respond uniformly over the whole image area.

Using a wide-field averaging meter for close-up photographs poses special problems. The indefinite field becomes especially hazardous and there is danger of casting the shadow of the meter itself on the subject if it is held close enough to read the small areas effectively. Frequently, too, the meter must be held at an unusual angle to avoid interfering with the camera, and may not "see" the subject surfaces in the same light as the camera does. If the object is lighted obliquely or if its surfaces are faceted or reflective, the problems are compounded.

Although reading the gray card as a substitute for the subject will alleviate most of these problems, it is not an ideal solution. The card itself is one more piece of equipment to carry and, if it is large enough

Below left: The reflectance meter saw this black doll as "a middle gray object in the dark" and overexposed it. You might prefer this rendering, but it isn't accurate. Below right: The incident meter, unaware of the subject tonality, exposed sufficiently to make a gray object, in that light condition, gray in the print. The black doll is, therefore, rendered as black, as it appears to the eye.

to be truly useful, it will be an awkward object to cope with. It is not an adequate substitute for a three-dimensional subject, either, and must be placed in the subject area with care to avoid uneven lighting and surface glare. In very small subject areas it may be impractical to include the card at all, although it is usually possible in such cases to find a similar light condition and make the reading there. In short, the gray card isn't perfect but it frequently can help a reflectance meter in situations where average luminance readings would be unreliable.

Since gray card readings don't depend on the tones and textures of the subject itself, the readings can be taken just as accurately—and frequently more conveniently—if the subject is not even present. In fact, for normal purposes, a gray card reading taken in a given condition of light will be adequate and accurate for *any* subject that may be placed there. The readings are not of the subject itself, as the usual reflectance readings are, but of the light available at the subject position; in other words, the *illuminance* or *incident light*.

Portrait of Richard Little Hawk Criss, by Doug Beasley. Doug used gray card substitute readings to determine exposure and development by the Incident Method. Courtesy of the photographer.

The Incident Meter

To retain the obvious virtues of the gray card method without its clumsiness, some canny soul invented the *incident meter*. It was a simple enough idea: it's really only a reflectance meter with a built-in gray card but, in this case, the gray card is in the form of a translucent plastic dome, which covers the meter cell. The translucency of the plastic is calculated to transmit middle gray light to the meter cell underneath, and the convex shape accepts light from the same sources and in the same relative intensities that a three-dimensional subject does. Placed in the subject position and pointed at the camera lens, the incident meter gives the same readings that a properly placed gray card will give with a reflectance meter. The incident meter's readings are also suitable for use "as is"—if the subject contrast and film development are normal.

The white plastic dome of an incident meter is equivalent to a built-in gray card.

It must be apparent by now that real control of print quality depends upon the production of excellent negatives which can be achieved only by accurate film exposure and development which, in turn, depend upon the extent of the subject luminance range, or SBR. If you are serious about controlling the photographic process, therefore, your first task is to determine the SBR. This is not always easy. The extremes of luminance—those values which will be recorded in the print as textured black and textured white—are usually small and frequently inaccessible areas of the subject. Sometimes, too, they may not actually be represented in the subject at all, but must be assumed to be there—and the exposure calculated to allow for them—in order to preserve the desired relationships among the other values.

Then there's the perception problem and it's a serious one. From the extreme range of subject luminance values that reach the eye, how does one go about selecting the relatively limited and specific range of tones that will constitute the selected image? And how precisely can the print values be predicted and visualized? The human eye and brain are amazingly capable of distinguishing between closely similar tones which are juxtaposed, but we have notoriously poor "tone memory" and have great difficulty in judging the value relationship of subject areas which are not seen side-by-side. To make matters worse, we are usually unaware that our perception is faulty; we see what we want to see and have almost no ability to "measure" light visually with objective accuracy.

Even with the aid of a spotmeter, decisions about subject gradation and luminance range are troublesome and require concentration and practice. In the subject area, which tone is near-white? Which one is middle gray? Which one do you want to register in the print as dark gray? What tone of gray will that white wall be in the print if you expose it one way, or another? What shade of gray will that red object turn into? No meter of any sort, nor any elaborate system of control, will free you up from decisions like these, and they are frequently perplexing! They are complicated, too, by meters that read larger or smaller areas of the subject than you think they're reading, or meters that are dazzled by light from outside their normal field of view, or meters whose sensitive cells are sluggish from being in the dark for a couple of days, or hypersensitive from a recent blast of intense light, or blind to some color, or paralyzed by cold, and so on. Some of these problems are common to all meters but some are the unique quirks of reflectance meters, including spotmeters. It makes sense, then, to re-think the incident meter, right?

But how can a meter which ignores the subject tell us anything about subject contrast? Remember that the luminance range of any subject results from the combination of two factors: subject *reflectance* (value, color, texture, and surface form) and *illumination*. A given shade of gray, for example, will give no reading on a meter, nor result in any image density on film, until it is illuminated. Then, as the illumination is increased, its luminance increases. Similarly, in a given light level, a dark-toned object will appear less bright than will a light-toned object. The third possibility, of course, is that a light-toned object in the dark may appear lighter than or darker than or the same tone as a dark-toned object in the light. Subject range, then, can result from the effect of various levels of illumination on objects of similar value, or from a variety of subject values and colors seen in the same illumination, or, most commonly, from the combined effect of varied subject values seen in varied light conditions.

Reflectance meters appraise subject luminance without regard to cause. Light objects in dark, dark objects in light, or gray objects in twilight are all the same to them as long as the total light energy reaching the cell surface is the same. Incident meters are responsive only to illumination level; the information they convey is essentially: this is how much light there is, you decide what the subject will look like. That's enough to start with: if we don't have to worry about the illumination we can concentrate on subject values and, fortunately, the range of tones that any nonluminous object can present to the camera is limited.

Determining the SBR with an Incident Meter

The maximum subject luminance range that can be produced by painting or staining or dyeing a material is rarely greater than 5 stops. There are a few exceptions: glossy photographic prints can reach a reflection density range of about 2.0, or 6⅔ stops, under ideal conditions, and spot-varnished duotone or gravure reproductions can also approach this range. These are unusual examples, though, and they aren't typical subject matter. The blackest black paint will seldom measure more than about 4½ stops darker than the whitest white paint, and the same is true of almost all colors and values, either natural or applied to surfaces. In everyday situations, even those few materials that might otherwise exhibit a greater inherent tonal range are dulled by surface dust or glare, reducing their visible contrast to 5 stops or less. All these illustrations assume, of course, that the light which illuminates the objects is uniform, without any areas of shade or shadow, and that the objects themselves are neither emitting nor transmitting light.

We can deduce from this that any object which is glare-free, shadow-free, and evenly illuminated will fit into a 5-stop luminance range—2 stops less than "normal." In practice, those 2 stops are supplied by local variations in illumination level, shadows, and surface reflection, to make up the 7 stops of the normal range.

I've already suggested that camera exposure should provide for all the tones, from black to white, whether they are actually present in the subject or not. Therefore, no subject that you intend to photograph without deliberate tonal distortion can be considered to have *less* than a 5-stop range. We've also agreed, I hope, that illumination variations will increase the subject range and must be included in its calculation. Therefore, it seems logical to assume that the subject luminance range can be estimated by adding the illuminance range—as measured with an incident meter—to the basic subject range of 5 stops. In practice this works surprisingly well.

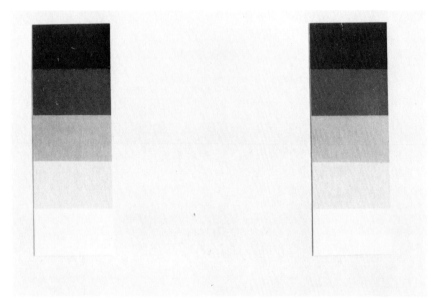

Each of these strips represents a subject range of 5 stops and they are illuminated evenly. Because film development was normal (suitable for a 7-stop range) the strips appear gray, without a satisfactory black tone.

When one of the strips is shaded so that its illuminance value is reduced by 2 stops, the total range of the subject is 7 stops and normal film development produces a full-scale print.

There is, of course, a problem that must be dealt with before theory can be reconciled with practice. As we mentioned earlier, a subject in uniform illumination can be assumed to have an SBR of 5 stops, and under these conditions an incident meter will give an unvarying reading regardless of its placement in the subject space. It would seem logical to use that meter reading in calculating the exposure (as recommended by Kodak for copy work) but—remember—the meter is calibrated to provide useful exposure over a range of about 7 stops: 3½ stops below and 3½ stops above the middle-gray point. Since the 5-stop subject needs only 2½ stops of effective range below and above middle gray, it's apparent that an uncompensated meter reading will provide about 1 stop more exposure than necessary.

This characteristic of the meter calibration is useful in most ordinary applications. It's sensible and practical, for example, to use an incident reading of a normal 7-stop subject without any adjustment (other than some alteration of the film speed setting to compensate for development). But other-than-normal subject ranges confront the meter with situations it's not equipped to deal with. One solution is to abandon the meter calculating scale entirely, and we'll discuss this in Chapter 10. Alternatively, we might recalibrate the meter itself (a complex and not very elegant solution) or—more practically—supply the meter with "doctored" information which will adjust its readings for any condition we choose.

This is the approach we'll take with the Incident System. By doubling all the film speed values derived from the film curves we can make a chart of "effective-film-speed-vs.-SBR" values, which will alter the meter's calibration from its normal 7-stop range to our desired 5-stop range. In other words, we'll trick the meter into underexposing 1 stop, thus reducing the middle-gray-to-detailed-black range from the "normal" 3½ stops to the desired 2½ stops.

You can make one further adjustment that will improve the accuracy of the Incident System. The effective film speed values found at the Dmin level of the curve family are comparable to the published ASA speeds but they aren't totally appropriate for incident metering, even when doubled. Because the meter reading represents a luminance value that is 2½ stops higher than the luminance of textured black (Dmin) in a normal 7-stop subject, the reading is correct only for that value—a medium-dark gray; but, since we expect the metered value to result in approximately the same negative density, regardless of SBR, it's apparent that this 2½-stop gap between the metering point and Dmin (on the exposure axis) is not appropriate for subjects of other than 7-stop range. For example, it places the metering point high up on the curve of a 5-stop subject, representing approximately a middle-gray value; a similar point on a 10-stop curve corresponds to a very dark gray value in the print.

Correcting these discrepancies is easy. Locate a point on the 7-stop curve at the density level corresponding to an exposure 2½ stops greater than that at Dmin (Fig. 6-1); this point will be used as the reference speed point in determining the relative speeds of the other curves in the family. Then construct a line through that point—and through the rest of the curve family—roughly parallel to the Dmin line.

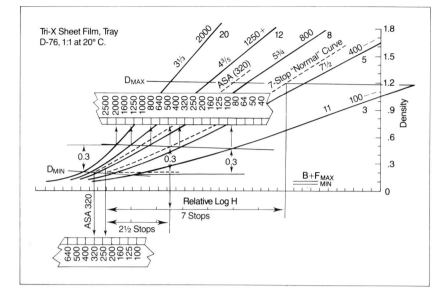

Tri-X Sheet Film, Tray
D-76, 1:1 at 20° C.

D_MAX

D_MIN

2500 2000 1600 1250 1000 800 640 500 400 320 250 200 160 100 80 64 50 40

2000 20 1250+ 12 800 8

3⅓ 4⅗ ASA (320) 5¾ 7-Stop "Normal" Curve 7½ 400 5

11 100

1.8
1.5
1.2
.9
.6
.3
0

Density

B+F_MAX / MIN

0.3   0.3   0.3

ASA 320

Relative Log H

2½ Stops   7 Stops

640 500 400 320 250 200 160 125 100

Figure 6-1. *Construct a new curve with an SBR of 7 stops (2.1) and mark it at a point corresponding to .75 (2½ stops) as measured from Dmin along the exposure axis. Measure the density range defined by this point on the curve (the vertical distance between the point and Dmin)—in this illustration the DR is 0.3. Apply this DR to the first and last curves in the family and connect the points with a straight line, as shown. Use the intersection of this line and the 7-stop curve as the new reference point for film speed determination, but assign it a value of twice the EFS of the 7-stop curve (as determined at the Dmin level). In this case, since Tri-X sheet film has an assigned speed of 320, the 7-stop curve is found to have an EFS of 250− (250 minus). Double this value to 500−, and align it (500−) on the film speed ruler with the reference point; then measure the effective film speeds as usual. This procedure will result in an apparently ridiculous series of film speeds, but they are appropriate for this metering method.*

The effective film speed of the 7-stop curve (rather than the ASA speed: see page 93) is used as the reference value and the other EFS values are found in the usual manner. Doubling these speeds, as described above, adjusts them for the System's unorthodox use of the incident meter.

Practically speaking, these changes are not vital ones. The Incident System was originally intended as a "quick and dirty" method of getting consistently usable negatives under a wide variety of condi-

Left: Metering the brightest illumination. This reading could have been taken right at the camera position if the meter were pointed in this same direction. Right: The meter reads 17 in the area of highest illuminance.

Left: Taking the low illumination reading. This reading could have been simulated at the camera position if the photographer had held the meter in his own shadow. Right: The meter reads 14 in the area of lowest illuminance. To find the SBR, subtract 14 from 17 to get 3 (stops); add to the basic 5 (stops) to find the total range—8 stops.

tions, and it will do that satisfactorily without adjustment. On the other hand, since these modifications are theoretically sound and increase the accuracy of the System considerably, they're worth incorporating and I recommend them. Bear in mind, though, that these inflated film speeds are not intended for use in any other system, and they should not be interpreted as an increase in the actual speed of the film. They're simply a system of numbers, deliberately distorted to compensate for what, for our purposes, is a flaw in the meter's calibration.

Using the Incident System

If you'll accept this concept you're ready to make pictures. We'll assume you'll use the Tri-X, D-76 1:1, Polycontrast combination we charted in the last chapter. Place your incident meter in the most brightly illuminated area of the subject space, point the meter cell at the camera, and note the reading. The film speed setting is not important at this point; it can be set on any value. You are concerned only with the actual illumination level, as indicated by the meter pointer. Now, place

Here's the print; the tones are rich and luminous. Photo by Tom Drew.

the meter in the darkest shadow area of the subject, point the cell at the camera, and note the reading. Subtract the shadow reading from the highlight reading—convert to stops if necessary—and add to 5. This is the total luminance range of the subject in stops, that is, its SBR.

To repeat, it isn't necessary to have an actual white object in the highlight-metered area, nor does it matter whether an actual black subject tone is present in the area metered for shadow detail. If you are striving for representational reproduction of the subject tones, it is necessary only to provide the correct exposure for those extremes in case they *are* present. If there aren't any blacks or whites in the subject, you probably don't want any to appear in the print.

Next, consult your effective film speed chart (Fig. 6-2) to find the film speed number appropriate for the SBR, and set it into the meter dial. Then, set the meter scale pointer on the light value you read in the shadow area, and select a suitable lens opening and shutter speed combination. Take the photograph, and mark the film holder with the SBR number for later identification. In the darkroom, consult your developing time chart (Fig. 6-3) and select the time appropriate for the SBR. Develop accordingly.

When you've made a few negatives, sampling a variety of light conditions, check them to see if they are consistent in density and contrast. If you have access to a densitometer, this will be a fairly simple procedure. The useful Dmin should read about 0.1-over-base-plus-fog and the DR should be about 1.0. Be sure you're appraising negative areas that represent the *useful extremes* of image tone, not the areas that should print solid black or pure white. If you don't have a densitometer, you'll have to rely on visual examination of the negatives and confirm your judgment by actually printing them.

Appraising Results Without a Densitometer

It's not possible to estimate densities very accurately but you can get a rough idea of image quality by inspecting the negatives on a light table. Since the unexposed margins of sheet film will normally have a density of about 0.1—representing B + F density—and since the image Dmin should be about 0.2, you can compare the image shadows with two layers of film base. The densities should appear similar. The highlight area should be medium to dark gray and well-detailed, and only the specular highlights—bright accents that should print completely white—should appear very dark gray or black. You can use a magazine page as a kind of densitometer, too. Lay the negative on the page, emulsion down, and see if you can read through the highlight densities. If the type shows clearly and you can read the words without difficulty, the density is probably less than 0.8. If the type is visible but not easily readable, the density is between about 0.8 and 1.0. A density of more than about 1.2 will obscure the type completely.

Next, make the best print you can, on normal contrast paper, without dodging, burning, or other manipulation. If the print requires much more than your usual exposure time, it indicates abnormally high negative density which, in turn, indicates film overexpo-

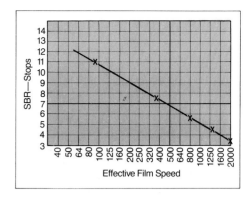

Figure 6-2. *This chart gives effective film speed values for use with the Incident System for any subject range when used with Tri-X sheet film, tray-developed with constant agitation in D-76, diluted 1:1, at 20°C, to produce negatives of 1.0 density range.*

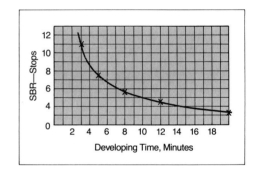

Figure 6-3. *This chart matches developing time to SBR and is intended to yield negatives of 1.0 DR when used with Tri-X sheet film, exposed as indicated in Figure 6-2, and tray-developed with constant agitation in D-76, diluted 1:1, at 20°C.*

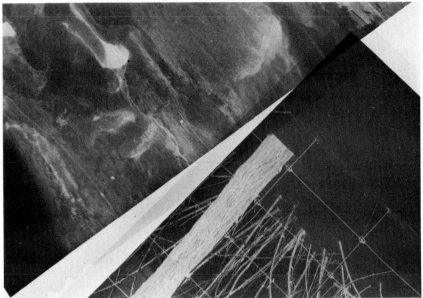

Comparing the density of the tree trunk with the density of the overlapping film edges indicates that the tree trunk has a safe and useful density of about 0.2 (about 0.1-over-B + F).

sure. If the image is excessively contrasty, it indicates overdevelopment of the film. Flat, gray prints indicate film underdevelopment. If the print does not contain the shadow details you expected to find, it may mean that the film was underexposed. Before you make that judgment, though, check the negative carefully to see if it contains the details you're looking for. If the negative shadows are adequately detailed, but the print shadows are opaque and featureless, it indicates overexposure of the print.

If you have photographed several subjects of different SBRs and the negatives are consistent and printable, the system is working, and both your metering technique and your calculated data are correct. If the negatives are consistent, but not printable—that is, if they are consistently too dense or thin or contrasty or flat—the system is working but your data or your metering technique are faulty. Consistency

It's difficult to read through negative densities of more than about 0.8. Negative density of the large dark area of the wall at left is about 0.65. The darkest area in the center reads about 1.1.

confirms the system and indicates that your processing is being adequately controlled. Inconsistent results probably indicate that you should review your negative developing procedure for careless errors or that you may be using the meter erratically.

Common Mistakes

Processing errors should be easy to discover and correct, but improper or inefficient use of the meter may be a little more difficult to recognize. Generally, photographers make two mistakes when using this Incident System the first few times: they tend to meter areas of apparent tonal extreme without distinguishing between *luminance* and *illuminance*. In other words, they are likely to assume that an area of the subject that looks dark in tone must represent a low level of incident light and that a bright-looking area must necessarily be brightly illuminated. Don't be fooled by appearances. It's essential to ignore subject color and value in establishing the metering points and consider only the level of illumination. Remember, this metering method is concerned only with light and shade; subject color and value are irrelevant as far as the meter is concerned.

Top left: Film overdevelopment will result in excessive contrast. This print was made from the normally exposed, overdeveloped negative (second negative, top row) in the array shown on p. 10. Top right: Underdevelopment will reduce negative density to some extent, but will be most obvious in reducing image contrast. This print was made from the normally exposed, underdeveloped negative (second negative, bottom row) on p. 10. Bottom left: Underexposure reduces image contrast somewhat but reduces shadow density in the negative most seriously. This print was made from the underexposed, normally developed negative (first negative, second row) on p. 10. Compared with the photo top right, this print is slightly more contrasty, but the shadows are less well detailed, giving the image an unpleasant murky appearance. Bottom right: Here's a normal print, made from the normally exposed, normally developed negative (center, p. 10). The fully detailed shadows and subtle highlight separation reproduce the hazy sunlight condition of the subject convincingly.

While learning to use the Incident System, beginners usually place the meter in unrealistically extreme conditions of illumination. To demonstrate this error, Peter Payette ignores his subject, Michael De-Vries, and stretches to place his meter in the deepest shade he can find. This extreme shadow reading will overexpose the film.

Here Pete compounds the exposure error by metering a brighter highlight than is appropriate for his subject. These two extreme meter readings suggest a much greater SBR than is desirable.

The overexposed, underdeveloped negative is dense and flat.

The other frequent mistake is one of interpretation. Beginners tend to meter the illumination extremes too extremely. They are likely to poke the meter into crevices of the subject which can't possibly be representative of "shadow illumination," and sometimes hold the meter closer to the light source than they should to represent any portion of the subject. These mistakes will produce unrealistically large SBR numbers which will result in overexposure and underdevelopment of the film, and the resulting negatives will be dense and low in contrast.

Flat, dense negatives are also likely when very contrasty subjects are encountered, even when the metering points are chosen correctly. The cause of this, which we'll discuss at length in Chapter 12, is *flare*, which increases shadow density and lowers contrast. Flare is not usually much of a problem when the subject contrast is low or normal, but

Left: A two-dimensional subject in flat light can usually be considered to have a range of 5 stops, but if you make the mistake of treating a three-dimensional subject that way you'll get harsh, contrasty results, as in this unflattering portrait of Judy Litschel. Right: The Incident System can cope with any subject condition if you use it intelligently. Take the highlight reading in the area of brightest illumination.

Left: You can't place the meter in the actual shadow areas, so shade the meter cell with your hand to simulate the shadow condition. This is the low reading. Right: Find the difference between the high and low readings, in stops, and add it to 5; that's the SBR. Consult your charts to find the effective film speed and development information. Here's the result: a better, more natural portrait of Judy.

its effect increases as the SBR increases and may become serious when the range exceeds 8 or 9 stops. Flare is not unique to the incident metering system; it's related to subject range and camera factors and is a potential hazard with any exposure system.

Incident Metering of Unusual Subjects

Beginners are frequently perplexed by subjects which don't have obvious illumination differences. A subject like a building in full sunlight is simple to meter because it's apparent that the sunlight represents one illumination extreme and the building shadow represents the other. Subjects in full shade, on the other hand, may seem to have no illumination range at all. Treating a shaded portrait subject, for example, as if it has only the minimum 5-stop range is unrealistic and will probably yield a harsh, contrasty negative. Remember, the 5-stop range minimum assumes no modulation of illumination of any sort. Every three-dimensional subject will exhibit some effects of light and shade and there will be discernible—if not obvious—shadows under the portrait subject's nose or chin or in the folds of clothing. Since you obviously can't position a meter in a nose shadow, you'll have to simulate the condition somehow. Hold the meter close to the subject and shade the cell with your hand until the shadows apparently match. Use that meter reading as the low-light extreme.

You'll have to resort to a similar technique when the subject is distant or inaccessible. For landscapes or cityscapes, assume the sunlight on the subject is as bright as it is at the camera position, if sky and weather conditions are similar. Meter it at the camera, being sure to point the meter cell in the same direction it would be facing if it were aimed at the camera from the subject position. Then simulate the subject shadow illumination by metering your own body shadow or stepping under a convenient tree. With practice you'll acquire skill in substitute metering and be able to use it to good effect. As a general rule, be sure to point the meter in a direction parallel to the lens axis and try to expose the cell to the same conditions of light that you observe at the subject location.

We've assumed that you want to represent the subject just as it is, yet this may not always be the case. Although distortions of subject contrast are easier to predict and produce with reflectance measurements than with incident metering, you *can* do some creative maneuvering with the incident meter and its associated data.

Creative Incident Metering

Consider, for example, a subject whose shadow areas contain only white and gray objects. Ordinary incident metering of the shadow illumination will produce a print with gray shadows, representing the values of the objects in shade. Your perception of the subject may not agree with this print interpretation. You may expect to see shadows which are dark in value because—especially in the print—gray

You can usually simulate the shadow conditions of distant subjects by shading the meter cell. Kearey Campbell demonstrates one simple method. This example simulates moderate shade, but may give an unrealistically high reading because of the strong reflection from Kearey's light-toned shirt.

Here's a safer technique for general use. Metering your own body shadow, as Kearey is doing here, simulates an open-shade condition very satisfactorily and is appropriate for this subject.

If the subject contains important details in heavily shaded areas, the meter must be shaded similarly. This low reading is too extreme for this subject and would lead to overexposure and underdevelopment of the negative.

69

shadows look weak and unnatural. If you want to correct for this, you'll have to darken the shadows and increase contrast by adjusting your metering technique or interpreting the meter readings. Manipulating the meter is easiest: just change the metering point. Move the meter out of the deep shadow area into a lighter area. Consider that reading to be the shadow value and proceed as usual. The immediate result will be a lower SBR number, which will call for less exposure and more development. The resulting negative will be thinner and more contrasty than a "normal" one. The extent of the change will depend upon how far you moved the meter out of the shadow area to take the reading. Remember, the meter's position in the dark area determines the point of realistic shadow rendering.

In other words, always place the meter in a light condition in which you'd like to have a black object rendered as textured black—if a black object were actually present in the subject. If no black object exists, but you still want a black area in the image, either reduce the indicated light reading to underexpose the shadows or meter an area which is sufficiently lighter than the "real shadows" to make them

Left: To show how meter placement can be used to control shadow density, Peter Payette prepares to photograph a light-toned metal sculpture. Mike DeVries, waiting with the incident meter, will take the high reading where he stands, holding the meter at head height. Right: Mike holds the meter in the darkest cavity he can find to take a low reading that will provide plenty of exposure for the deepest shadows and suggest a long SBR for relatively short development time.

Left: The overexposed, underdeveloped negative produces a slightly flat print with excellent shadow separation but rather weak accent blacks. Right: By placing the meter in an area of open shade, Mike reduces the SBR and shadow exposure. With less exposure and more development, the negative is more contrasty with less shadow density.

appear suitably dark by comparison. This will require good observation and judgment, of course, but you wouldn't want photography to be completely automatic and impersonal, would you?

It's probably less likely that you'll ever want to raise the value of a gray object in the brightest illumination to white, but if you do, the method is the same. Simply take the highlight reading in a light condition that is less bright so the "real highlight" area will be overexposed. In all cases, when the subject range is manipulated by moving the metering points this way, the system automatically compensates for both exposure and development. No further calculation is required.

Making Adjustments

When you've worked out the initial problems and are getting consistent results, it's time to fine tune the data. If the negatives are consistently too thin or too dense—and you're sure your metering procedures are not at fault—you can probably correct the difficulty by changing your effective film speed chart without having to go back to

The resulting print is "snappier" with richer blacks and more brilliant highlight rendition.

the film curves. Estimate the extent of the exposure error and revise the chart to compensate for it. For example, if you estimate that you're consistently overexposing by 1 stop, shift the calibration numbers on the x-axis to the left by three ASA numbers—such as from 160 to 320 (Fig. 6-4). Use the newly indicated speeds for another series of negatives. After one or two such adjustments the chart should be accurate and reliable for you, whether or not the numbers agree with anyone else's or the manufacturer's published film speeds.

If contrast is a problem it will be best to recalculate the development chart from the characteristic curves. You *can* make an approximate correction by shifting the working chart curve, but it's risky. It doesn't take long to make a new chart from the original data, so take heart and go back to the old drawing board.

You can estimate the necessary amount of correction by trying various paper grades to see what contrast is best. If your negatives print best on #1 paper, it indicates that either your original data were based on an unrealistically high ES value or, for some reason, your enlarger and your processing techniques are combining to produce more than normal contrast. In either case, the cure is simple. Redraw the Dmax line on your film curve family to produce a lower negative DR. If, as in the example above, you want to reduce contrast by one paper grade, subtract about 0.15 from the original DR. Since the DR value we've used in previous illustrations is 1.0, that will mean a change to 0.85. Then reconstruct the SBRs and redraw the developing time chart, using the new values. Use the same technique to correct for consistently low contrast. If you get best results by printing on #3 paper, increase the original negative DR by 0.15.

If your experience is typical, you will find this system—and the other systems which we'll consider—generally reliable and consistent. In fact, they may be almost too reliable. Occasionally you may find that you've succeeded in recording the subject values but the result is not pleasing. The print, in other words, is not the picture you saw in your mind's eye. There isn't any simple cure for problems of judgment. You'll have to become accustomed to the difference between camera vision and human perception and train yourself to see photographically. This is, in fact, the biggest single problem you'll have to face.

Although there are no formulas for improving your perception, there are a few hints which may be helpful. As you study the subject try not to be influenced by tonal extremes or areas of contrast outside the actual picture area. It may help at first to view the subject through a mask opening cut in a piece of gray cardboard. Then, within this defined subject area, consciously identify the extremes of value which you want to record as black and white in the print. Compare the other values with these extremes to determine their relative value. Try to visualize the print image as you examine the subject, relating the subject values and colors to print values. Then be sure to meter the correct extremes of illumination to achieve the results you've visualized.

You should now have a good understanding of sensitometric principles and their application to the practical problems of exposure

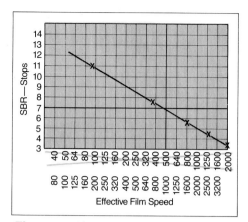

Figure 6-4. *If careful field testing indicates consistent exposure error, it can be corrected by re-calibrating the EFS chart. In this example the chart calibration has been changed to compensate for overexposure of 1 stop.*

Viewing your subject area through a gray cardboard mask may help you decide on a composition and will provide a neutral reference for the various subject values.

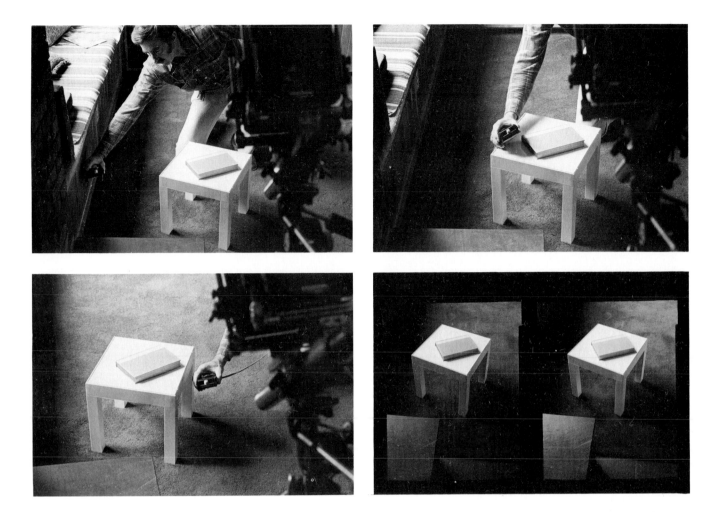

and development. You should also comprehend the function of the various types of exposure meters and be able to interpret their readings. The virtues of the Incident System of metering should be apparent, and I hope you'll experiment with the system to exploit its potential. In the next chapter we'll briefly review the case for luminance metering. Then, briefly surveying the conventional methods of testing, we'll consider the famous Zone System to see what it is, how it works, and what it can do.

Highlight value can be controlled by meter placement, too. Top left: First meter the deepest shade in which you want detail to appear. This reading remains unchanged regardless of variations in the meter placement for highlight reading. Top right: This meter placement will provide a tone on the white table top; its incident light reading was 2½ stops higher than the shadow reading for an SBR of 7½ stops. Bottom left: This reading, taken beyond the table, away from the light source, is only 2 stops higher than the shadow reading, for an SBR of 7 stops. This calls for more development, and the increased image contrast makes the table top nearly pure white while leaving the shadows almost unaffected. Bottom right: Since both exposure and development are influenced by changes in the SBR, negative Dmin is maintained at an optimum level and the negatives can be printed together without manipulation. The 7½-stop SBR is at left; the 7-stop SBR at right.

The Zone System Summarized

As I've mentioned before, the normal pointer on the calculating dial of a hand-held reflectance meter represents the midpoint of the subject luminance range. Theoretically, it identifies the subject luminance value that will be recorded in the print as a mid-tone gray (the actual gray value will depend on your handling of the process variables). If you're comfortable with the idea that all the normal subject luminance values can be recorded in the print, you'll see, I think, that every subject luminance has a *corresponding* print tone. You can trace a low value of luminance through the process to a specific dark gray in the print, for example, and, similarly, trace any high value of subject luminance to its corresponding light gray print value.

Relating Subject Luminances to Print Values

You'll find it easy to demonstrate this relationship if you identify these print gray values right on the meter dial so they can be seen opposite the luminance values they're related to. With a gray scale of this sort on your meter dial you'll find it easy to visualize the approximate print tone that corresponds to any area of a normal 7-stop range subject you care to meter.

In addition, you can see that since proper exposure results when you meter a middle-gray area of the subject and set its luminance value opposite the middle-gray patch (corresponding to the meter pointer) on the meter's reference gray scale, you can arrive at the same correct exposure by metering a dark area of the subject and placing its luminance value over a correspondingly dark patch on the meter gray scale. This is also true if the luminance value of a light area of the subject is positioned opposite the appropriate light gray patch, or, in fact, if *any* subject luminance value is paired with its matching value on the meter reference gray scale.

This pencilled gray scale, attached to the meter scale with rubber cement, indicates the approximate values of print gray that correspond with the various luminance values of the normal subject.

75

To repeat, in this system, the meter normal pointer stands for print middle gray and is appropriate for use when you are metering a middle-gray area of the subject or when the metered area contains an even mix of light and dark tones which average middle gray. The normal pointer is only one of 7 "pointers"—the 7 gray scale patches. You can use any one of them to determine proper film exposure if you align it with the metered luminance value of a similar subject tone. Match a dark subject value with a dark scale patch, a light subject value with a light scale patch or a medium subject value with the middle gray scale patch (the normal meter pointer); in every case the meter should indicate the same camera settings if the subject luminance range is the normal 7 stops.

A further advantage of working with the visible gray scale is the possibility of deliberately distorting subject values in their translation into print tones. Since each of the 7 meter gray patches indicates the print tone you can expect normally from the subject luminance it is set on, you can darken a too-light subject area by setting its luminance value on a darker gray patch, or lighten a too-dark subject area by setting its luminance value on a lighter section of the meter gray scale. This simple approach to print tone control is reliable only if the subject luminance range is the normal 7 stops, and if film development is normal—as established by test or experience.

The Zone System

These principles—that a subject value can be translated into any desired print tone by meter placement, and the general concept of visualization of the print tones before the film is exposed—are the foundations on which Ansel Adams' famous Zone System is built. Adams worked out the details of the system with Fred Archer in the 1940s and explained them in his book *The Negative*. Minor White's *Zone System Manual*, published in 1953, and *The New Zone System Manual*, co-authored with Richard Zakia and Peter Lorenz, published in 1976, expanded and embellished Adams' concepts.

But there are as many opinions about what the Zone System is, what it can do, and how it should be used, as there are authors and teachers. This is true, in part, because Adams' original explanation— although generally sound and remarkably advanced for its time—is rather loosely organized and somewhat difficult to follow. Also, because the system is based on empirical test methods, it isn't easy to derive complete and accurate data or to define the procedures with precision.

Simply stated, the Zone System attempts to combine visualization, exposure, and development to produce a negative which contains a record of the subject, modified by the aesthetic judgment and technical skill of the photographer. If all goes well, the final print represents an interpretation or expression of the essence of the subject rather than a mere confirmation of its existence. It is, of course, possible to produce interpretive or expressive images without using the Zone System or any other codified approach, but the use of a reliable system helps. It can relieve photographers of many on-the-spot calculations and technical decisions, facilitate their visual appraisal of the subject, and increase their chances of success.

The Zones

The brief discussion of luminance metering which opened this chapter introduced some of the basic techniques used in the Zone System. You can calibrate your own meter for Zone System use, if you want to, by affixing numbered gray scale patches to its dial. Roman numerals are always used to identify the Zones—Adams called them "exposure zones"—and each number identifies a specific print gray value. They are usually defined like this:

Zone		
	0	Pure black; no print detail, no texture
	I	First indication of tone above black
	II	Textured, but not detailed black
	III	Very dark gray
	IV	Dark gray
	V	Middle gray; 18% reflectance
	VI	Light gray
	VII	Very light gray
	VIII	Near-white, textured but not detailed
	IX	Pure paper white

The N-Numbers

When the subject range is normal, each Zone corresponds to a stop, as indicated on your meter's luminance scale. To repeat an example, metering a very dark gray area in the subject and lining up its luminance value with the Zone III patch on the meter scale—called "placing" the luminance in Zone III—will provide normal exposure for all the other subject values as well. The luminance value for some light gray in the subject will then "fall" in Zone VI and a near-white will fall in Zone VIII, where they normally belong. To state it another way, when a selected low value is placed in its appropriate zone on the meter scale and a selected high value falls in its proper zone, the subject range is normal and the appropriate development condition or "N-number" is "Normal" or "N." When the low value is placed properly but the high value does not fall in its normal zone, the subject contrast is higher or lower than normal and the development must be adjusted.

Here we enter one of the several areas of disagreement. Adams suggests placing Zone I values and checking to see where Zone VI values "fall." White generally concurs but, in at least one instance, recommends placing Zone III values and checking Zone VII values to see where they fall. Other sources may suggest placing Zone II and checking Zone VIII, or Zone II and Zone VII, or some other pairing. The

Meter scales differ considerably so you may have some difficulty designing a gray scale to fit your meter. The Pentax Spotmeter dial (top) is easily adapted. The SBC Luna-Pro (middle) can be fitted with a scale like this one. The Zone Dial ZX-1 (bottom), shown attached to the CalcuLight meter, is an accessory.

zones selected are not particularly important; you can work with any pair. It is important not to interchange them, though, because N-numbers suitable for use with one pair of zones may not be appropriate for another pair.

Development times suitable for abnormal subject ranges are determined from the position of the high luminance value. For example, if a very dark gray subject luminance value is placed correctly in Zone III, but a very light gray luminance value falls short of its normal Zone VII position on the meter scale and lands instead in Zone VI, it indicates that the subject contrast is abnormally low. The film must, therefore, be developed longer than normal to restore the contrast in the negative. In other words, the development increase is intended to expand the subject contrast sufficiently to push the high luminance into Zone VII where it belongs.

Since this example represents a range "expansion" of one zone—from VI to VII—the required developing time—whatever it is—is referred to as "N + 1," or "Normal, plus one zone." If the high value falls in Zone V instead of its normal Zone VII, the expansion development required is N + 2. On the other hand, if the value falls in Zone IX instead of Zone VII, "compaction" or "contraction" development—less than normal—is required. Since, in this case, the required reduction in range is two zones, the N-number is "N − 2" or "Normal, minus two zones." Again, there is no general agreement about the reference zones for determining expansions and compactions. Pick your authority and abide by his or her recommendations.

Until the publication of *The New Zone System Manual*, Zone System authors had generally dismissed as insignificant the effect of varied development on effective film speed. The determination of an effective speed for personal use has always been a feature of the system, however, and—like most conventional Zone System information—it is arrived at by trial and error.

Summary of Conventional Test Methods

The method generally recommended goes something like this: first, establish a "standard printing time" by comparing test prints of the negative base-plus-fog density to a "maximum paper black" sample print. The minimum exposure time required to produce a full black in this test is considered the standard. Then expose a series of films to a standard gray card, using the normal ASA rating of the film and taking care not to introduce exposure errors due to reciprocity effects or bellows extension factor. The exposures are varied by full-stop increments in order to produce a full range of zone values. It is assumed that if normal exposure and development produce a Zone V gray, reducing that exposure by 1, 2, 3, 4, and 5 stops will produce Zones IV, III, II, I, and 0, respectively. Similarly, overexposures of 1, 2, 3, and 4 stops, developed normally, will presumably yield Zones VI, VII, VIII, and IX, respectively.

When these negatives are printed, using the standard printing time, the darker prints are examined to see whether they fall into the proper zones. If the Zone I print is determined to be a Zone I value, and if the Zone V print is a Zone V value, the film speed is considered to be normal. If the Zone I print is actually a Zone II value, it indicates greater-than-normal exposure and the effective film speed is then arbitrarily increased by—typically—1 stop. A Zone II exposure found to be a Zone I value calls for a speed decrease of 1 stop. If the Zone I value is correct but the Zone V value is not, it implies that development is not normal. The tests must then be rerun, after some estimated correction in developing time.

We have treated the conventional testing procedures briefly for two reasons: first, they have been described exhaustively elsewhere and, second, this approach to analysis of film and developer characteristics can hardly be recommended for either efficiency or accuracy.

In use, the Zone System is similar to the Incident System except for the obvious difference in metering procedure. In both systems the subject luminance range must be measured or estimated before exposure or development can be determined, and in both the actual exposure is based on some sort of shadow reading. Although the Incident System is simpler and more nearly foolproof, the Zone System is much better suited to visualization of the subject luminance relationships and creative control of the image tones. Each has its advantages and you will become more versatile if you learn both.

You should now have a general understanding of the Zone System and what it can do. You should also be aware that it's possible to acquire accurate exposure and development information without going through the usual tortuous procedures. Much of the work, in fact, we've already done. In the next chapter we'll consult the characteristic curves again and extract from them the information needed to make the Zone System work as effectively as possible.

Zone System Data: The Curve Family Revisited

I hope you're not troubled by the apparent discrepancy between the 7-stop SBR which we've considered normal, and the 9- and 10-zone (stop) ranges described by Adams and White. The explanation is rather simple. The 9-zone range results from including the accent tones of black and white in the normal range, while the 7-stop SBR excludes the extremes and deals only with the textured or detailed tones corresponding to Zones II through VIII (Fig. 8-1).

The 10-zone scale is based on the assumption that some useful image tone is available in Zone I and that Zone 0 represents true black (Fig. 8-2). Actually, this is a reasonable belief. The 0.1 over B + F Dmin point on the film curve is merely an officially approved limit (by ANSI) and should not be taken to mean that tonality ceases abruptly there. It merely marks a point chosen because contrast is decreasing rapidly in

Figure 8-1. *The 7-zone and 9-zone SBRs are different ways of describing the same negative. The 7-zone range simply omits black and white, which are included in the 9-zone description. The 10-zone range considers Zone I to be usefully separated from Zone 0, and includes Zone 0 as accent black. In both 7- and 9-zone ranges Zones 0 and I are considered to be black and Zones IX and above are considered to be white.*

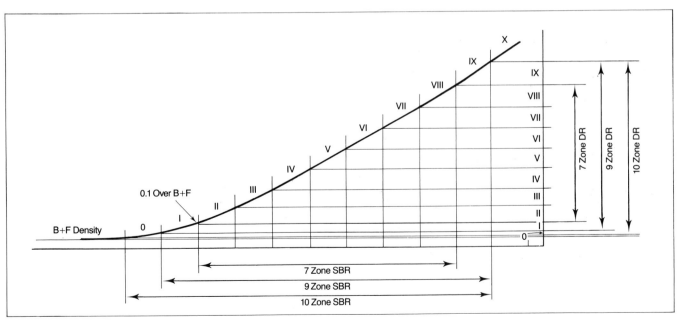

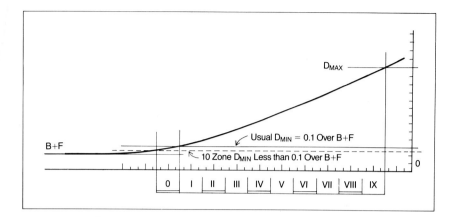

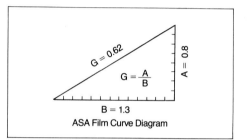

Figure 8-2. The usual version of the 10-zone range includes some of the region below the normal Dmin limit (0.1 over B + F). Even this is an arbitrary limit. There is still some image information below Zone 0 but it can hardly be called "useful."

the toe region of the curve and a limit has to be established somewhere. If you feel, as Adams did, that there is some subtle tonal separation to be exploited in the negative densities below 0.1, feel free to include them in your own definition of "normal."

The Normal Range in Zones

There is good reason, though, for limiting the "normal" range to the 7-stop, 9-zone maximum or even somewhat less. This has to do with film speeds and meter calibration standards, both of which have been largely ignored in Zone System literature. The ASA speeds, as you know, are based on the rather unrealistic average gradient of about 0.62, arrived at by dividing the specified DR of 0.8 by the similarly specified logE range of 1.3 (Fig. 8-3). If we translate these numbers into practical values and substitute for 0.8 the more reasonable negative DR of 1.0, the related logE range becomes about 1.61, or roughly 5⅔ stops (Fig. 8-4). Alternatively, if we specify our normal logE range of 2.1 in place of the ASA value of 1.3, the resulting DR becomes about 1.3 (Fig. 8-5). In other words, the ASA speeds are applicable only if a 5⅔-stop range is considered normal, or if a low-contrast paper is used to print negatives made from a 7-stop subject, or, possibly, for some low-contrast printing condition such as the use of a cold-light diffusion enlarger.

The ANSI standard for exposure meter calibration is similarly unrelated to Zone System practice. Some Zone System literature refers to Zone I—and in one case Zone 0—as being located at 0.1-over-base-plus-fog. If this were true, the normal metering point—middle gray, or Zone V—would necessarily be separated from the 0.1 Dmin by some 4 or 5 stops. In fact, meters calibrated according to ANSI standards effectively place the normal pointer only slightly more than 3 stops above the standard speed point (Fig. 8-6). In other words, ANSI apparently considers Dmin to fall slightly below the middle of *Zone II* in the normal subject range. Considering that meters and films generally conform to these two ANSI standards, it's easy to see why Zone System users have learned to think of any luminance under about Zone III as

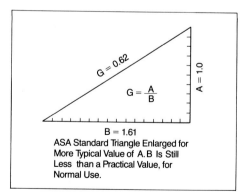

Figure 8-3. The standard ASA film curve, reduced to simplified form. We'll refer to it as the "ASA standard triangle."

ASA Standard Triangle Enlarged for More Typical Value of A. B Is Still Less than a Practical Value, for Normal Use.

Figure 8-4. The ASA standard triangle gradient value of 0.62 is unrealistically high for normal use; as demonstrated here, an abnormally short subject range (about 5⅓ stops) is sufficient to produce a negative of normal DR.

practically unusable without some film speed adjustment or some arbitrary increase in indicated exposure. If no such adjustment is made, underexposures in the order of 1 or 2 stops are highly likely for normal subjects and even greater errors are indicated for long-range subjects.

Even the 7-stop range is slightly optimistic, compared to the ANSI ideal, but it's close enough to be well within the normal tolerances of the process (Fig. 8-6). We'll continue to use it as the basis for curve analysis in spite of the fact that it necessitates de-rating the ASA film speeds by about ⅓ stop, as discussed in Chapter 3.

In Figure 8-7 our 7-stop SBR is related to the commonly accepted 9-zone range. Again, the extreme zones I and IX fall beyond the limits of the SBR and therefore represent the accent tones of black and white. Zone V coincides with the middle stop and Zones II and VIII match the first and last stops in the range. Since we'll need measuring points in these zones for our analysis, we'll consider them to fall in the *center* of each zone. The center of Zone V, therefore, marks the exact center of the 7-stop range and, although the Zone II and Zone VIII center marks do not indicate the outside limits of the SBR, the *outer boundaries* of these zones do.

Remember, the luminance values increase gradually and continuously along the exposure axis and our lines and marks are placed arbitrarily. Although we usually think of them as discrete grays, each zone includes a *range* of luminances which blend into the adjoining zones without any visible line of separation.

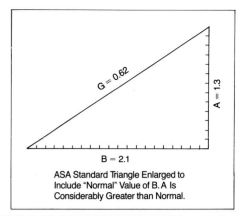

Figure 8-5. *If the ASA gradient is applied to a normal 7-stop SBR the resulting negative has an abnormally large DR.*

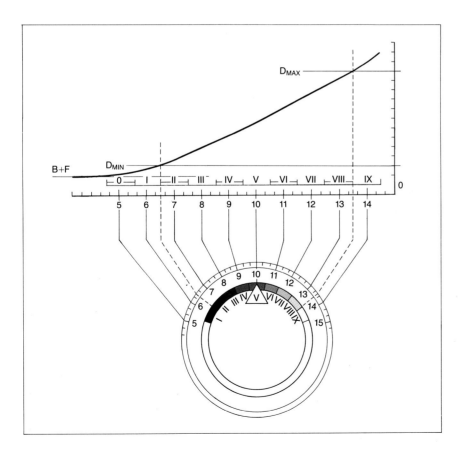

Figure 8-6. *The 7-zone concept is practical and realistic. It matches the conventional meter calibration standards quite closely but still requires an adjustment of the ASA film speed values for optimum exposure. This concept is identical with the 9-zone scale in which the extreme accent tones—black and white—are included (as Zones I and IX) but are acknowledged to fall outside the range of useful gradation.*

What a "Zone" Is—And Isn't

As you have probably inferred by now, the term *zone* is used rather loosely and there is some confusion about what it really means. Adams cleverly labelled them "exposure zones" and was careful to distinguish between subject zones, negative values, and print values. In more recent literature the distinction is not always so clear. Two descriptions are probably uncontestable: a full range print contains *all the* zones as actual gray values; and the subject luminances are called zones when they are visualized as being analogous to the print zone grays. It should be apparent that print zones are *not* equivalent to stops, since the total reflection density range of the print rarely exceeds 2.0, and is typically less than that. Even if the zones represented uniform divisions of the print density range, which they don't, the average print zone would amount to only about ¾ of a stop. In fact, they are not at all uniform. The middle print zones turn out to be considerably greater than 1 stop long, while the extreme zones are relatively small fractions of a stop long (Fig. 8-8). The negative zones aren't equal to stops either, nor are they equal to each other. The shape of the characteristic curve tends to shorten the lower zones somewhat, and the normal negative DR of approximately 1.0 limits the average length of the individual zones to about .14, or ½ stop (Fig. 8-9).

If I have seemed to put unnecessary emphasis on the distinction between stops and zones, it's because it's important that the zones be thought of as *visual* divisions of the subject and image values rather than invariable, measurable increments of density or reflectance. It's very useful to carry a mental image of the zone values, but remember that translating the tones of the subject into the tones you ultimately see in the print can involve any number of combinations of subject, negative, and paper variables. At any stage of the process, stops can be relied upon to remain constant and measurable as representative of density or logE values of 0.3; zones have no consistent numerical value but they do consistently symbolize specific tones of gray.

You can base your subject luminance range measurements for determination of the N-numbers on any pair of zones you like but unless you have reason to do otherwise, I'll suggest using Zones III and VII. These two zones are spaced widely enough to give a reasonably

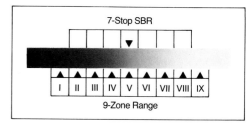

Figure 8-7. The 7-stop SBR compared with the 9-zone range.

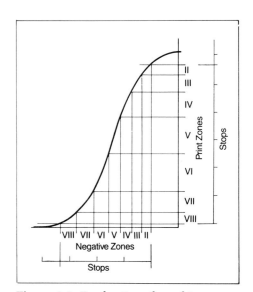

Figure 8-8. By the time the subject zones have been translated into print densities they no longer equal stops.

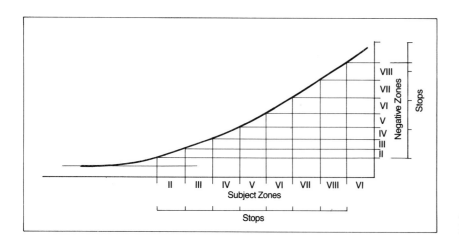

Figure 8-9. Negative zones aren't equivalent to stops either.

accurate indication of the total subject range but they also represent values which are easier to identify and measure than more extreme zones are likely to be. In the curve analyses which follow, we'll determine N-numbers by metering Zones III and VII and assume that the working data we derive are intended to produce full-scale print images in which all the normal zones from I (black) to IX (white) are represented. This print range should be attainable from negatives whose DR of 1.0 includes the *textured* Zones II through VIII—which implies, of course, that the *total* negative DR, including Zones I and IX, is somewhat greater than 1.0.

Since a full-range print image must contain all 7 textured zones plus the extremes, it follows that those same zones must be assumed to be present in the subject because, otherwise, visualization of the print values would be impossible. Furthermore, since the normal subject range consists of 7 *equal* zones—each equal to 1 stop—subjects of unusual range will also contain 7 zones, equal to each other, but *not* stops. In other words, because a normal 7-stop subject has seven zones, each of which is $1/7$ of the total range, a 5-stop subject, for example, also contains 7 zones, each of which is $1/7$ of the total 5 stops—or $5/7$ of a stop. By the same reasoning, a 12-stop subject should have 7 zones, each $12/7$ of a stop (Fig. 8-10).

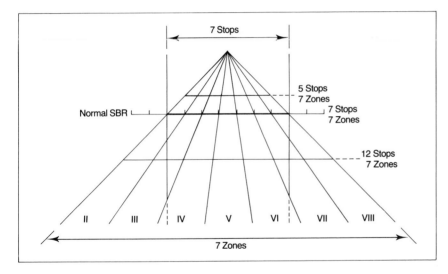

Figure 8-10. Zones equal stops only when the subject range is normal.

Zone System Curve Analysis

If you'll accept that concept let's turn to the curve family and apply it. Assemble your drawing instruments and some graph paper (or a worksheet from the Workbook, page 41) and follow along as we go through the analysis.

First, locate the Dmin points on each curve toe, at a density level of 0.1 over B + F, and connect them to form the Dmin line (Fig. 8-11). Then locate the Dmax points on each curve at a level 1.0 greater than the Dmin value for that curve, and draw the Dmax line (Fig. 8-12). Now draw light vertical lines through the Dmin and Dmax points on one of the curves and extend them well below the base line of the graph. Now draw a horizontal line between the verticals to represent the SBR.

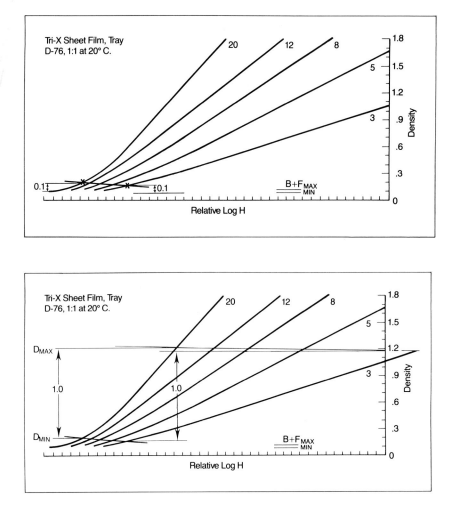

Figure 8-11. *Locate on the first and last curves the point that represents a density of 0.1-over-base-plus-fog. Connect these two points with a straight line to establish Dmin for the curve family.*

Figure 8-12. *Locate on the first and last curves the points on each that represent a density of 1.0 over the Dmin value for that curve. Connect these points with a straight line to establish Dmax for the curve family. It will probably be necessary to extend one or more of the curves beyond the graph boundary to accomplish this, as shown here.*

In the Incident System analysis we simply measured the SBR line in logE numbers or stops, but for Zone System use we need N-numbers. To find them, it's necessary to divide the SBR into zones. One way to do this is to walk off 7 equal segments of the SBR line with a pair of dividers. You can also accomplish the necessary division with a ruler; place the ruler across the space between the vertical lines and angle it as necessary to position 7 inch-spaces—or half-inch spaces, or centimeter-spaces, or whatever—precisely between the lines (Fig. 8-13). Then transfer the spaces to the SBR line, using your triangle and T square for accuracy. When you have divided the first SBR into its 7 zones, label them from left to right "II" through "VIII," and mark the exact centers of Zones III and VII.

Finding the N-Numbers

To find the N-number, you'll need to compare the length of the subject range between Zones III and VII with the normal spacing of 4 stops. An easy way to do this is to make a paper ruler, several inches long, marked in full-stop increments as measured along the exposure axis of the graph. If you prefer, you can cut out and use the "zone

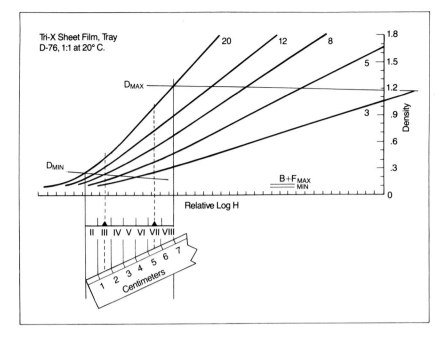

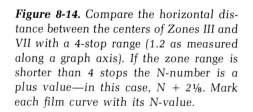

Figure 8-13. Angle a ruler until seven of its divisions span the SBR. Mark the 7 zones and indicate the centers of Zones III and VII.

finder" ruler printed on the worksheet, page 55 of the Workbook. Align it with the range you want to measure and count the stops difference between that range and the normal 4-stop range indicated on the ruler. The difference between them is the N-number. If the subject range is greater than 4 stops the number has a "minus" value. If the range is shorter than 4 stops, the N-number has a "plus" value. In this example, the horizontal distance between the midpoints of Zones III and VII measures 1⅞ stops; it is 2⅛ stops less than 4, so the N-number is N + 2⅛ (Fig. 8-14). In Figure 8-15, the measured range between III and VII is 6⅓ stops; the difference is 2⅓ stops and the number must be "minus"—therefore, N − 2⅓. Following this procedure, complete the calibration of the other curves and compare your finished drawing with Figure 8-16.

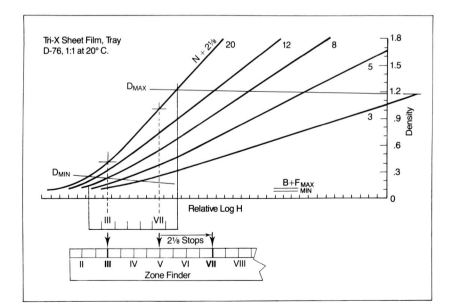

Figure 8-14. Compare the horizontal distance between the centers of Zones III and VII with a 4-stop range (1.2 as measured along a graph axis). If the zone range is shorter than 4 stops the N-number is a plus value—in this case, N + 2⅛. Mark each film curve with its N-value.

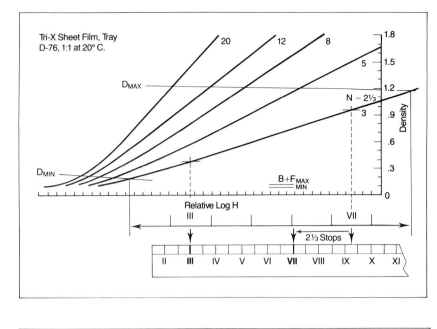

Figure 8-15. In this case the 4 zones between III and VII measure 6⅓ stops long. That's 2⅓ stops more than the normal 4-stop range so the N-number is N − 2⅓.

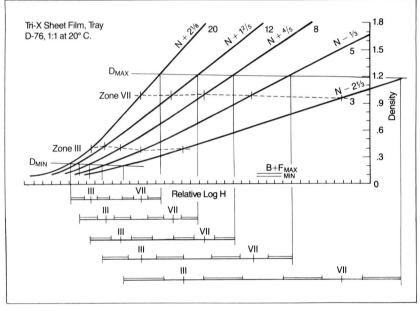

Figure 8-16. Here are the film curves with all zone construction lines shown and the curves labelled.

Now that you're familiar with the procedure, you can use another worksheet to find N-numbers for other values of DR or for other reference zones, or both. If you work with other zones, be sure to compare their measured ranges with the correct normal range in stops. For example, if you use Zones II and VIII, the normal spacing is 6 stops, not 4; and if you select Zones I and VI, as Adams has suggested, be sure to measure them against a 5-stop standard. If you do find N-numbers for other zone pairs, be careful to label the charts clearly to avoid confusion. The N-numbers will be quite different for the different zone pairs and cannot be interchanged without causing errors in your working data.

Effective Film Speeds: Review

The film speeds calculated for use with the Incident System are not appropriate for Zone System use either, because of the difference in metering methods. Let's take a few minutes to compare them. Incident meters are calibrated to provide a range of approximately 3½ stops between the normal pointer and the lower limit of useful exposure (which corresponds to the useful Dmin point on the normal film curve). When an incident meter is used to measure the average illumination of a normal subject, it will recommend an exposure that translates the subject mid-value into print middle gray and at the same time translates the darkest detailed or textured area of the subject into a perceptibly detailed or textured near-black in the print (Fig. 8-17a).

For subjects of other than the normal 7-stop range, an averaged incident reading will suggest exposure settings that will still render the subject mid-value as print middle gray, but the shadow areas will not be recorded as satisfactorily. Consider, for example, a subject range of 10 stops. An incident reading based on average illumination will place the normal pointer at mid-scale—5 stops above the lower limit of shadow detail and 5 stops below the boundary between useful highlight detail and pure accent white. The suggested camera settings, however, will provide an exposure sufficient to record only 3½ stops of subject range below the normal pointer position. This leaves 1½ stops of desirable shadow detail outside the recorded range—underexposed—and the print will show these areas as solid black (b). If the film is developed normally—that is, appropriately for an SBR of 7 stops—highlight details will also fall outside the normal density range of the negative and will not be printable on normal contrast paper. If the film development is reduced to maintain normal negative contrast and preserve these highlights, the resulting reduction in effective film speed will degrade the shadows still further.

At short SBRs the opposite effect occurs. Assuming normal film development, the meter will provide an exposure recommendation sufficient to overexpose the subject shadows while underexposing the highlights (c). The print—if made on normal contrast paper—will be weak and gray. Increasing film development to restore highlight contrast will also increase the effective film speed, overexposing the shadows still further.

The Incident System previously described compensates for these problems by basing the camera settings on adjusted meter readings taken in *shadow* illumination (Fig. 8-18a, b). This procedure provides adequate shadow exposure regardless of subject range. Highlight density and overall contrast are controlled by varying development, as determined by the SBR (Fig. 8-18c). The attendant variations in effective film speed are compensated for by adjusting the ASA setting on the meter dial to a value appropriate for the SBR (Fig. 8-18d).

In the Incident System the effective film speeds are derived from the film curves at a level somewhat below their mid-density points. It's important to realize, however, that the film exposure sufficient to provide this desired level of minimum density is *not* the exposure in-

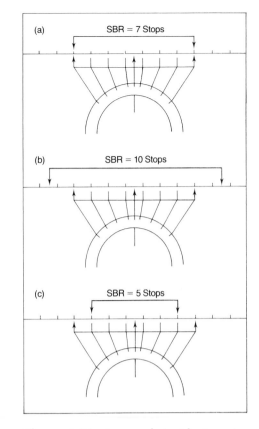

Figure 8-17. *Averaged incident meter readings adjust the exposure for an average value of subject range. This is fine for subjects of normal range (a), but it won't be correct for subjects of very long range (b), or very short range (c), unless some adjustments in film exposure and development are made.*

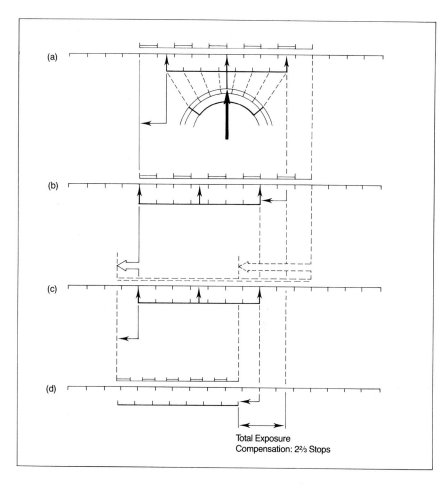

(a)

(b)

(c)

(d)

Total Exposure
Compensation: 2⅔ Stops

Figure 8-18. In (a) a subject of 10-stop range is diagrammed as it might relate to an incident meter reading. If given normal exposure and development, about 1½ stops of shadow detail and 1½ stops of highlight detail will not be recorded usefully. In (b) the meter has been set to include the shadow details (by increasing the camera exposure by 1½ stops) but normal development will now exclude 3 stops of highlight detail. In (c) development has been reduced to compress the 10-stop SBR to the normal 7 stops. This has the effect of reducing highlight exposure by about 4⅙ stops but also reduces the shadow exposure by 1⅙ stops. In (d) a further exposure increase is required to restore adequate shadow exposure. This increase is sufficient to shift the meter range 1⅙ stops to coincide with the subject range. The entire subject is now recorded on the film; negative density and contrast are normal. The total exposure compensation has been about 2⅔ stops.

tended by the meter: the meter recommendation is normally about 3½ stops higher than the exposure required to produce negative Dmin (but you'll recall we reduced it to 2½ stops by doubling the effective film speeds—see Chapter 6 if you've forgotten why this was done).

Because Dmin placement is critical and because the meter reading normally relates only to middle gray, Dmin has to be placed by a kind of remote control. It can't be metered directly—with an incident meter, at least—but we can manipulate it at arm's length, so to speak. We get it to coincide with the desired 0.1 over B + F speed point by jockeying it into position at the end of its (adjusted) 2½-stop handle. The other system adjustments—positioning the meter in the subject space and the selection of effective film speed and development—are all intended to keep Dmin where we've placed it while bringing the other image tones into line.

Like the Incident System, the Zone System is designed to provide a more or less uniform value of negative Dmin, regardless of subject range, but it approaches the problem a little differently. Although it is sometimes possible to base exposure calculation on Dmin values—by reading a subject luminance value midway between Zone I and Zone II and placing that reading 3½ stops below the normal pointer on the meter, in practice this is almost never done. There are at least two reasons for this: first, it's not easy to perceive luminance differences in the very low range and zone recognition may be somewhat inaccurate and inconsistent there (it's often useful to consider these zones, though, during previsualization). The second and more compelling reason is that the boundary between Zones I and II defines a tone which is almost accent black and this, by definition, is likely to be represented in the subject by very small areas which can be difficult to meter accurately. This is not always true, of course; some subjects do contain large areas of dark tone which should be rendered as near-black in the print for best effect.

Although it would be most accurate to base the Zone System working data on measurements of the extremes of subject luminance—Zones I and IX, for example—it is generally not practical to do so. Not even a spotmeter, with its relatively narrow field of view, is capable of probing the folds and crevices of most subjects for accurate measurement of accent blacks; and specular highlights—those glittering reflections on metal corners and glass edges, for example—defy measurement of any sort. Because of this, the workable limits for spotmeter use are probably Zones II and VIII. If you use an ordinary wide-field reflectance meter, you'll be wise to work even more conservatively, using Zones III and VII.

In most discussions of Zone System use, it's implied that once the N-numbers have been determined they can be applied to any pair of zones, more or less at the whim of the photographer. Within the limits of accuracy which conventional testing provides, this is probably true;

Some subjects contain large areas of dark tone which should be rendered near-black for best effect.

but it is not true if you are seeking more precise control. Exposure and development information based on N-numbers derived from Zones II and VIII, for example, is not accurate for use with Zones III and VII, or I and VI, or any other zone pairs. This is so because Zone System exposures are not determined *directly* from the measured subject luminance values. Instead, the pointer is deliberately set at some value *higher* than the luminance reading so the selected subject luminance will be underexposed to some specific degree.

If you've selected Zone III as your low standard, you'll read the luminance value of some dark gray area of the subject, then mentally increase it by 2 stops, and set the meter pointer on this higher selected value. Here—as in the Incident System—the standard exposure point (in this case, Zone III) is positioned by remote control. You can only work *directly* with the normal (Zone V) meter readings but *they* aren't significant; what you're interested in (Zone III) is tied to Zone V by a short rope—in this case, 2 stops long.

This procedure is convenient and accurate for subjects of the normal 7-stop range because that means that zones and stops are equal, and a deliberate underexposure of 2 stops can indeed shift the luminance value from Zone V to Zone III. For other subject ranges, however (and this is a nicety generally ignored by Zone System workers), zones and stops are *not* equal, and a 2-stop shift of the luminance value on the meter dial will *not* move that value 2 zones (Fig. 8-19).

There are two ways of dealing with this problem (other than

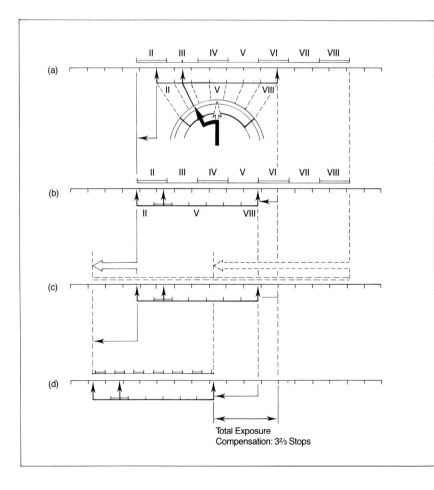

Figure 8-19. In (a) a Zone III area of a 12⅓-stop subject has been metered and placed in Zone III on the meter dial. With this meter setting and normal development, approximately 1⅙ stops of shadow detail and about 4⅙ stops of highlight detail will not be adequately recorded on the negative. In (b) although Zone System exposure compensation is actually accomplished in a single step (by calculating EFS values on the low zone instead of the conventional Dmin) it really is a two-stage process: first, the meter setting is altered to include the subject shadows—an exposure increase of 1⅙ stops in this case, which now excludes about 5⅓ stops of highlight information. In (c) development is reduced to compress 7 long zones of the subject into 7 zones of normal (1 stop) length. This drastically reduces the effective film speed and requires a final compensation (d) of about 2½ stops increase in exposure. Total exposure increase required in this hypothetical example is about 3⅔ stops.

simply dismissing it, of course). If you can devise some convenient method for stretching or shrinking the strip of 7 reference grays (zones) on your meter scale—so it can be made to match an SBR of any number of stops—your system accuracy will be improved and exposure compensation is conventional. Since this is hardly practical, however, it's preferable to modify the exposure correction itself. This is ridiculously simple: calculate the effective film speeds for the various subject ranges at the Zone III (or whatever low zone reference you prefer) density level of the curves, rather than the usual speed points—0.1 over B + F (Fig. 8-20). Although this change in procedure may seem to leave the negative Dmin free to wander from its optimum position, it is actually appropriate and effective. When the system is calibrated this way, and used responsibly, negative density and contrast can be maintained with remarkable consistency, regardless of subject range.

Shifting the Speed Points

If the reason for moving the speed points up to the Zone III (or whatever) level puzzles you, don't feel you've missed something. After all, a film curve which has an apparent film speed of, say, 80 at the Dmin level should continue to have a speed of 80 throughout its length, shouldn't it? How can it be 80 at 0.1 density and 32, for example, at 0.3 or 0.4? Well, remember, film speed officially applies only to the 0.1 density point on the standard ASA curve, for which SBR, DR, and—by implication—$\overline{G}$ are specified. This official speed point serves as a basic reference for calculating the relative speeds of all the other curves; as you will recall, from the discussion beginning on page 47, the EFS value of any curve in the family can be found by measuring the distance between its speed point (its point of intersection with the Dmin line) and the ASA speed point, along the exposure axis of the graph. The speeds thus found are accurate indicators of the EFS values *at the Dmin level*, but it's obvious that the spacing between the curves (which accounts for the speed differences) increases at higher density levels. It follows, therefore, that the relative speeds must change as image density changes.

I was convinced, originally, that the ASA curve was a suitable standard for calculating effective film speeds at any and all density levels but Chris Leggo, a friend and fellow sensitometry enthusiast, has pointed out that relative effective film speeds for points at density levels above Dmin should be calculated from the "normal" 7-stop curve. Chris is right; although the ASA speeds are officially *defined* by the standard ASA curve, they are actually *implemented* by being set into the meter dial; and meters—as I've pointed out several times—are designed to consider a 7-stop range as "normal." Since the meter always equates zones with stops, and since it's demonstrable that the same exposure results from pairing any luminance value with its matching zone "pointer" on the meter dial, it's apparent that it's the 7-stop curve that maintains a constant speed—not the ASA curve, as I have previously written. It's important to realize, however, that the

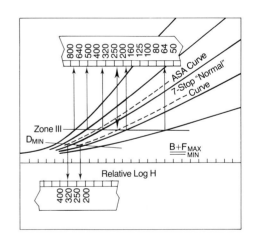

Figure 8-20. Calculate EFS values for Zone System use on the selected low zone level. First construct a "normal" 7-stop curve (see Figs. 8-21 and 8-22) and determine its EFS by comparing it with the ASA curve at the Dmin level, as shown. Then use the intersection of the 7-stop curve and the selected low zone line as the reference speed point for finding the other EFS values. In this illustration the new reference speed is found to be 250−.

93

actual speed of the 7-stop curve *must be determined first, by reference to the ASA curve at the official speed point level—0.1 over B + F* (Fig. 8-20).

In practice, the difference in speeds calculated from the 7-stop curve and those calculated from the ASA curve, is not great at density levels at or below about Zone III, but there are significant and increasing differences at higher levels. Although it would be unusual to base EFS values on these higher levels, it's wise to avoid any possibility of serious error and use the 7-stop curve as the reference for all levels other than the official Dmin at 0.1 over B + F.

Figure 8-21 illustrates a method for constructing the necessary 7-stop curve in the curve family. It's similar in every respect to the procedure we followed in finding the ASA curve (pp. 47-50) except that the dimensions of the triangle are different. The base dimension must be 2.1, of course, but the altitude must match your desired negative DR. In the illustration we've used 1.0 as the DR value and the triangle is shown positioned so that its lower vertex touches the Dmin line; the base is parallel to the x-axis of the graph; and the acute vertices are spaced proportionately between the same pair of film curves. As is the case with the ASA triangle, only one position in the curve family will satisfy these requirements. When the triangle is properly placed, mark the positions of its vertices and sketch in a curve that will connect the marks while matching the character of the neighboring curves (Fig. 8-22).

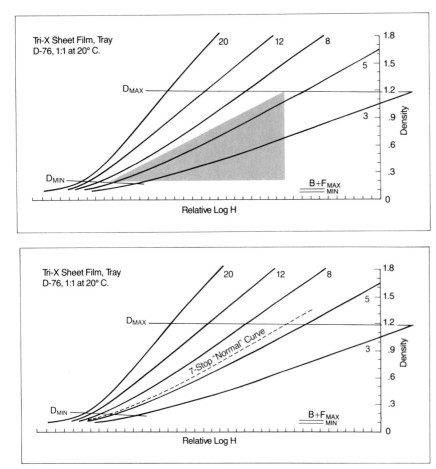

Figure 8-21. The 7-stop "normal" curve can be located just as the ASA curve was, using a triangle of the appropriate dimensions. The base must measure 2.1 (7 stops) and the altitude must equal your chosen value of negative DR. The altitude is 1.0 in this illustration.

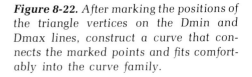

Figure 8-22. After marking the positions of the triangle vertices on the Dmin and Dmax lines, construct a curve that connects the marked points and fits comfortably into the curve family.

Figures 8-23a, b, and c illustrate the differences in EFS values that result from measurement at different density levels, and demonstrate the reason why Zone System calibrations for different zone pairs may not be interchangeable. Notice that the effective speed of the 7-stop

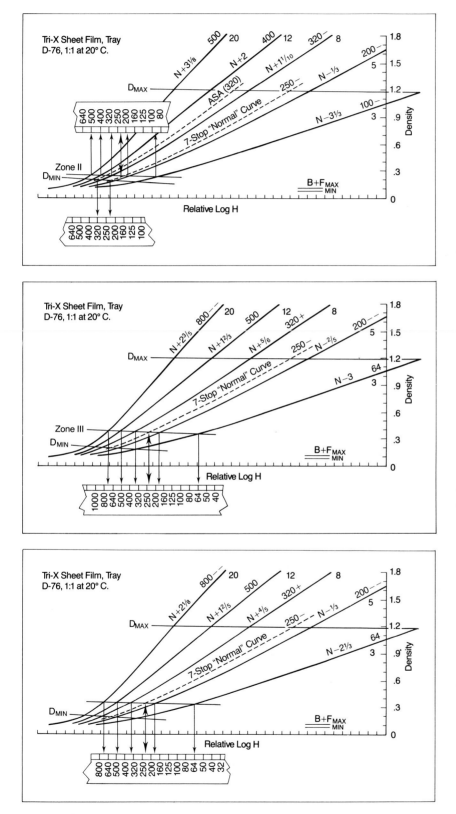

Figure 8-23a. *This illustration shows the relationship between EFS values and luminance range (expressed in N-numbers) when the chosen limits are Zones II and VIII. First the EFS value of the normal (7-stop) curve is found by measuring from the ASA speed point at the Dmin level. Then the intersection of the normal curve and the Zone II (center) line becomes the reference speed point for calibrating the other curves.*

Figure 8-23b. *In this illustration the selected zones are III and VIII. Compare both the EFS values and N-numbers with those shown in Figures 8-23a and 8-23c.*

Figure 8-23c. *When Zones III and VII are used for calibration, the EFS values match those in Figure 8-23b, but the N-numbers are different. This is because the EFS values are determined solely by the low zone, but the N-numbers are determined mainly by the "spread" (difference in stops) between the selected zones. In this case the spread is 4 stops; in the illustration above the spread is 5 stops.*

"normal" curve remains the same in all cases but that the EFS values of all the other curves (each representing a specific N-number) vary as the zone level changes. You can see that rather serious exposure errors can result if EFS values are not related closely to subject range as expressed by the N-numbers.

Zone System Working Curves

Now we can chart the working curves. Using a chart from page 53 in the Workbook, plot the values of effective film speed for Zone III versus the N-numbers, just as you did when working with the Incident System. Use the calibrated film speed ruler printed on the worksheet on page 55 in the Workbook to find the speed values for the individual curves, measuring from the Zone III density on the 7-stop curve, as in Figure 8-24a. Be sure to keep the measuring ruler parallel to the graph base line. Connect the points on the chart with a smooth curve and label it clearly "III" to indicate that its values apply *only* to Zone III placement on the meter scale. Do not use these film speeds for any other zone placement.

Next, plot the developing times for the curves against their respective N-numbers and connect those points with a smooth line. Then compare your charts with Figures 8-24 a, b, and c.

You can use another worksheet to work with other values of DR or derive N-numbers based on other zone pairs. Remember, if you do compile data for other zone pairs, label them clearly to avoid possible confusion in the field. The N-numbers are accurate only for their own zone-pairs; they are *not* interchangeable.

The data charts are derived from the same Tri-X, D-76 1:1 combination that we used for the Incident System calibration. Although there is always the possibility that your equipment and work habits will produce results different from someone else's, you should be able to get acceptable negatives by using this information just as it is. Why not try it? Load up some holders with Tri-X and pack up your camera, meter, and related equipment. The only addition to your usual gear will be the effective film speed chart. Cut it out of your worksheet or transcribe it onto a piece of graph paper, and paste it onto your meter case or the camera back where it will be easily available.

Field Testing: Visualization

We haven't discussed flare effects or reciprocity failure at any length, so you should probably try to avoid them for the time being. Pick a not-too-contrasty subject in reasonably good light, and establish your composition on the camera's ground glass, so you'll know what luminance values you have to consider. Then look directly at the subject, concentrating on the selected area and trying to ignore any extremes of luminance that appear outside it. Within the subject area

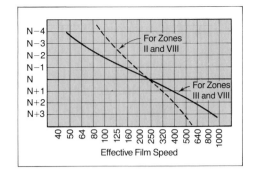

Figure 8-24a. *Values of EFS calculated from one pair of zones will not be suitable for use with any other pair, as is illustrated here. Notice that the EFS lines cross at 250−, the EFS value of the 7-stop curve and the reference value from which the others are found.*

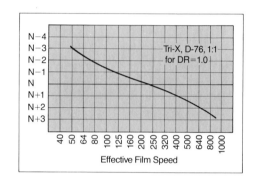

Figure 8-24b. *This chart gives values of EFS for use with Tri-X sheet film developed in D-76, 1:1; the calibration zones are III and VII. Compare this curve with those in Fig. 8-24a.*

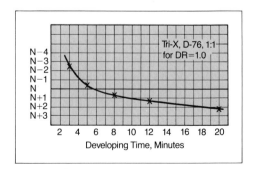

Figure 8-24c. *The developing time chart for Zones III and VII. Tri-X, D-76, diluted 1:1.*

look for the reference extremes: identify print white—Zone IX—and print black—Zone I—and check them carefully against other similar values—Zones VIII and II, for example—to be sure you're not assigning too much or too little of the total range to each extreme.

Then identify a middle gray value—Zone V—and compare it visually with each of the extremes to be certain it really is a middle tone. Finally, consider the areas of the subject which are most important and compare them to your three reference values to determine what zones they represent. When you have decided what the subject zones are, decide whether you want to record them as they are, or modify the value relationships in some way.

Changes of this sort will necessarily be restricted. You can increase or decrease overall contrast by arbitrarily changing the zone assignment of one area relative to another; and you can place a particular subject area in some desired zone without significantly affecting overall contrast if you are willing to have all the other values shift along with it. Manipulations of a single zone, without affecting others, are practically impossible, or at least so limited as to be insignificant.

Now continue your study of the subject while checking your zone selections against luminance readings of the various areas. You will probably find some of your zone choices inconsistent with their measured luminance values. If so, you'll have to change your visualized image of the subject to coincide with harsh reality, or consider some other interpretation of the scene. When you have arrived at some zone assignments which satisfy both you and your meter, determine the N-number as follows (this assumes you have calibrated your working charts for Zones III and VII).

Metering to Find the N-Number

Meter the Zone III area and place its luminance value on the Zone III patch on your meter dial. The ASA setting is not important; for now, leave it wherever it is. Then meter the Zone VII area of the subject and notice where its luminance value falls in relation to the Zone VII patch on the meter dial. Count the stops between the luminance value position and the Zone VII patch, correct to the nearest ⅓ stop. That number is the N-number. If the subject luminance value is higher than the indicated value at the Zone VII patch on the meter scale—that is, if the subject range between III and VII is greater than 4 stops—the N-number is a minus number. If the subject value is lower than the indicated meter value at the Zone VII patch, the subject range between III and VII is less than 4 stops and the N-number is a plus number.

The photo on page 98 demonstrates this procedure. The subject luminance values are given as: Zone III, 5; Zone VII, 10⅓. Luminance value 5 is shown placed in Zone III and luminance value 10⅓ is shown to fall 1⅓ stops above Zone VII on the meter scale. Because it's necessary to count down-scale to reach Zone VII, the number is minus; N − 1⅓. (See Fig. 8-25.)

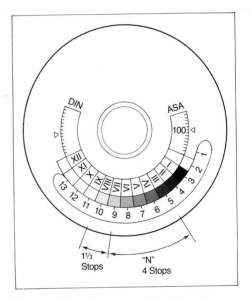

Figure 8-25. Here a subject luminance value of 5 is shown placed in Zone III. If the subject were normal, the luminance value 9 would fall in Zone VII and no further adjustment would be necessary. In this case, however, the luminance value 10⅓ is supposed to fall in Zone VII. Since the luminance range is 1⅓ stops greater than it should be, development must be shortened to "compact" the 5⅓ stop range back to the normal 4 stops so the development condition is said to be "N − 1⅓."

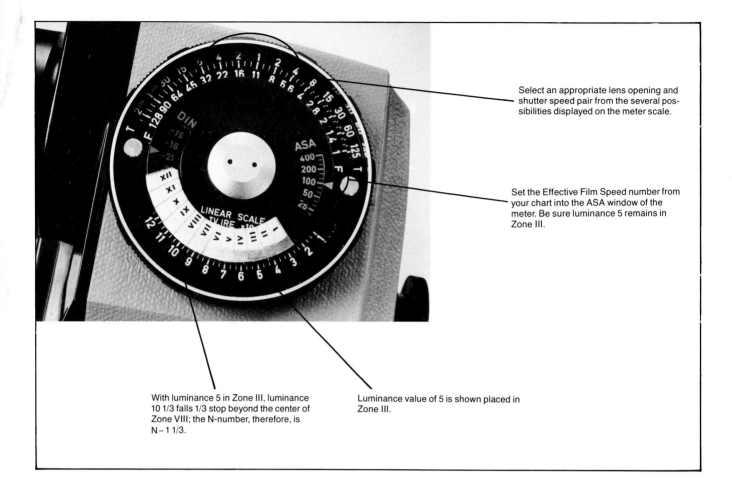

Select an appropriate lens opening and shutter speed pair from the several possibilities displayed on the meter scale.

Set the Effective Film Speed number from your chart into the ASA window of the meter. Be sure luminance 5 remains in Zone III.

With luminance 5 in Zone III, luminance 10 1/3 falls 1/3 stop beyond the center of Zone VIII; the N-number, therefore, is N – 1 1/3.

Luminance value of 5 is shown placed in Zone III.

This procedure is the conventional one and is presented because it dramatizes visually the so-called "compaction" of the luminance range, required to restore it to normal. In practice, you may prefer to do the calculating in your head. Subtract the Zone III luminance value from the Zone VII value and compare the number of stops so found with the standard 4. If the number is greater than 4, the difference is minus; if less than 4, the difference is plus. In the example above, 5 subtracted from 10⅓ is 5⅓; 5⅓ is 1⅓ greater than 4 so the N-number is N − 1⅓. This procedure will not work with meters calibrated in foot-lamberts or candles-per-square-foot, or other similar values, until they have been converted to stops.

Using the Chart Information

When you have determined the N-number using either method, consult the effective film speed chart (Fig. 8-24b), and set the indicated speed number into the meter in place of the regular ASA number. Then, if necessary, realign the low luminance reading with the Zone III patch, and select the camera settings. Apply any pertinent exposure factors and make the exposure. Mark the holder with the N-number or record it so you can identify individual exposures later. When you are back in the darkroom, consult your developing time chart (Fig. 8-24c) for the appropriate time for each film, and process the individual sheets accordingly.

Print the negatives on normal paper without local controls. When the prints are dry, inspect them in good light to see how closely they match your visualization. Check them critically also for total range, and for shadow and highlight detailing. If some of the images match your expectations but some don't, consider it due to lack of experience in visualization, zone estimation, or lack of familiarity with this procedure. Experience should improve your average. If none of the pictures are quite right, examine them to identify the problem, and to determine whether they all display the same symptoms. If they are consistently too contrasty or not contrasty enough, you can probably salvage these negatives by printing them on other grades of paper. For future use, though, the developing chart curve should be altered, as discussed in the trouble-shooting procedures for the Incident System. Refer to those instructions, also, for ways to deal with consistent over- or under-exposure (see pp. 69-71).

When you have appraised the print results thoroughly and made the necessary corrections in your working chart data, make a new series of pictures. Concentrate on the subject zone assignments. This stage of the process is the most important and the one most likely to give you trouble. It is also your opportunity to be creative. To a considerable degree your zone decisions will determine whether the picture is great or merely satisfactory.

CHAPTER
9

How to Run Your Own Film and Paper Tests

You can't practice sensitometry effectively without a densitometer. In fact, you should have two: one for reflection (print) densities and one for transmission (negative) densities. New, professional-quality instruments suitable for both these uses will probably cost $1500.00 or more. This is clearly an unrealistic expense for the average photographer and one reason why sensitometry has never been a very popular subject.

Luckily, you don't need an instrument of professional quality, nor do you need all the features of the expensive models. You can get along very nicely with an instrument of modest range, calibrated for reasonable accuracy. You don't need voltage stabilized circuitry, automatic range switching, programmable color channels, or digital readout. You do need to be able to read relatively small and accurately defined areas of your negatives and prints, and the readings, if not absolutely accurate, should at least be repeatable.

Densitometer Options

There are a number of options. You may be able to find a moderately priced used densitometer, but think this over carefully before you buy. It will almost certainly cost several hundred dollars if it's in working order, and if it isn't in good shape you don't want it. Densitometers are not easily repaired, and the repairs are not cheap. Don't buy an old vacuum-tube model which "just needs a little fixing up," and don't buy an imported one, either. You'll find parts for well-known domestic brands hard enough to come by.

The electronics revolution that has given us solar-powered wristwatches and briefcase-sized computers has affected densitometers too. There are several basic black-and-white transmission densitometers on the market in the $400 to $600 price range and at least one for under $200. One of these may be suitable for your purposes and your budget.

A third alternative is to design and build your own. Don't consider this unless you are familiar with hobby-type electronic circuits and are handy with tools. It's not a project for beginners but if you feel competent to undertake it, you can make a serviceable instrument for about $50. The photograph below shows a home-built transmission densitometer and its accessory reflection density unit.

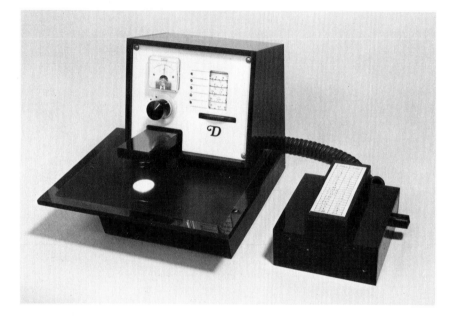

A home-built densitometer.

Adapt Your Light Meter

A fourth—and excellent—alternative is to use your hand-held exposure meter. Most meters can be adapted with results ranging from acceptable to excellent. This is possible because some of the essential features of a densitometer are provided by the exposure meters themselves, especially spotmeters, without requiring any modification. In other words, a densitometer *is* basically a light meter designed for specialized use.

In conventional designs the negative to be analyzed is placed on an illuminated area of the densitometer table and the light transmitted by the test area is picked up by a photo-cell. The light reading is processed electronically and displayed in log numbers as negative density. The test area of the negative can be varied by changing "apertures" in the table. These aperture discs are opaque except for a small central hole and therefore confine the illuminated area of the negative to a circle, typically about 1 to 3 millimeters in diameter.

Before use, a densitometer must be adjusted to show zero density. The instrument will then indicate a density reading if the light dims for any reason, including a reduction in the line voltage. Professional densitometers avoid this potential error by electronically stabilizing the lamp voltage and the instrument power supply—an important

The reading area of a commercial densitometer with a gray scale density positioned over the reading aperture. In use, the nose piece is forced down over the sample density to exclude all light except that which is transmitted through the aperture.

feature for maintaining laboratory standards of accuracy and repeatability.

A densitometer for personal use doesn't need this degree of accuracy. An error of as much as ⅓ stop (0.1 density) is not particularly serious if it is consistent and repeatable. It is much more important that the instrument be capable of reading a small area—preferably a millimeter or so in diameter—and that the reading area be clearly and accurately defined. An overall range of at least 10 stops, or 3.0, is desirable and there must be some way to convert the meter readings if they are not given directly in density values. Home-built densitometers and meter conversions are capable of satisfying all these requirements.

The simplest practical meter adapter I know of is the experimental model shown; it was designed to accept the standard CdS Luna-Pro and will provide a useful reading range of more than 3.0. The aperture diameter is about 1½ mm. and is in the upper part of the device rather than in the table. Although this increases the effective size of the aperture somewhat, it facilitates positioning the negative because the translucent table insert illuminates a large area of the negative around the actual reading area. The area that will be measured is indicated by a small circle marked in the plastic. When the meter is lowered onto the negative to make the reading, the aperture falls directly over the indicated area. If the hinge is well-made and free from lateral play, the aperture positioning is quite precise. The meter will respond to the average density of the negative image tones within a circular area about 2 mm. in diameter. A similar conversion unit for the Calcu-Light meter is shown; many other popular meters can be similarly adapted.

In use, the densitometer table is simply taped down to a desk top with the translucent insert overhanging the edge by 1 or 2 inches. Place a light on the floor directly under the insert so it is evenly illuminated; raise the light up to register about 14 or 15 on the Luna-Pro scale with no negative in place. The actual luminance value is not important but it must be recorded accurately because it represents zero density. Be careful not to move either the meter table or the light while making your readings, to avoid altering the zero calibration.

When a negative is positioned over the illuminated insert, the meter reading will drop to a lower value—take note of this value also. The negative density can be calculated by counting the stops between the two readings and multiplying by 0.3, but that's the hard way. If you copy the calculator scales printed on page 29 of the Workbook on Kodalith film, print them as suggested and assemble the device as shown, you can convert the meter readings to densities directly, without any figuring. This calculator—suitably calibrated—will work equally well with any other meter conversion which is designed to provide fully diffused illumination for the negative.

Densitometer adapters for meters like the CdS Luna-Pro will provide useful density readings but are inconvenient to use. Furthermore, the high and low scales of the meter may not be in exact agreement in their area of overlap, and some error is possible. In spite of these drawbacks, you can measure your test negatives and draw respectable curves with a meter of this kind if you prefer not to invest in another one.

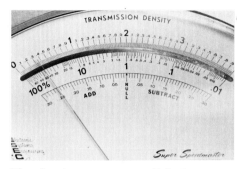

The densitometer meter dial showing a density reading of 0.36 on the upper scale.

A densitometer conversion unit for the CdS Luna-Pro. Sealing the fiber-optic chamber is the last construction step. See Workbook, page 25.

A densitometer conversion unit for the CalcuLight meter. The calculator dial beside it is used to convert the meter readings to values of density.

Spotmeter Conversion

If you own a good spotmeter, or plan to buy one, you can adapt it easily for both transmission and reflection density readings. In some respects a converted spotmeter rivals or even surpasses professional densitometers. If well-designed and carefully constructed, it will read a negative area of about 1 mm. in diameter and the reading area can be selected with greater precision than any conventional densitometer design will allow. The instrument will cover a range of more than 3.6 (12 stops) and can be converted from transmission to reflection readings instantaneously. Its accuracy and repeatability are well within useful limits. Finally, it is smaller, lighter, and more flexible than any commercially available densitometer, and substantially less expensive than any equally capable one.

An early experimental design is pictured. This model, designed to accommodate the Asahi Spotmeter V, is rather crudely constructed but functions very satisfactorily. It will read transmission densities of more than 3.0 and covers an area of about 1 mm. It is accurate and repeatable within about 0.1 for both transmission and reflection densities. A more refined conversion unit, this one for the Minolta Autospot II, is also shown. It's probable that any other spotmeter can be similarly converted if the basic design is modified to match the meter dimensions. See the Workbook, part 1, for plans and construction details. When you've bought or built or borrowed a densitometer you can proceed with your personal testing.

A CdS Luna-Pro meter in its adapter, set up to measure transmission densities.

There are several ways to convert meter readings to density values; here are two devices which will do it conveniently. See pages 28 and 29 in the Workbook for more details.

The Step Tablet

You'll need one other item—a film step tablet. I suggest the Kodak Photographic Step Tablet #2, which covers the range from about 0.05 to about 3.05 in 21 steps. Get the uncalibrated model and calibrate it yourself with your own densitometer; the calibrated version is much more expensive and not necessary.

Prepare the step tablet for use by numbering each step neatly near one edge, using opaque drawing ink. Begin with the least dense step; number it 1 and number the others in sequence. The darkest step at the extreme end of the strip will be number 21. Now read the densities of the steps and record the values. You'll refer to them frequently during your tests.

Materials testing must be done carefully if the resulting data are to be used effectively. Keep careful records so you can repeat the tests without significant variation after a few weeks or months. Also try to control the critical stages of the procedures; you can relax a little during the steps that are not likely to affect image quality.

For calibration purposes it's best to begin at the end of the process and work backwards. The print image, after all, is the goal of the entire process.

The original spotmeter densitometer; it was crude but it worked.

Paper Testing: Finding Your Scale Index (SI)

The first step is to decide what kind of prints you like. If your printing style is already well established and you have some prints which you consider to be of excellent quality, you can work with them. If not, select a fine, normal negative from your files and make several prints of it. Try any brands and surfaces of paper that seem promising. Don't worry about different developers at this point and don't vary the dilution or the developing time; just give normal development. Make the best-looking prints you can and bracket each one by making one a little lighter and one a little darker than the one you think will be best. Fix them in fresh hypo, preferably using two baths in sequence, for not more than 4 or 5 minutes total and keep the fixing time uniform. Use a hypo clearing bath and wash the prints thoroughly; then air-dry them on clean screens, or a clean white cloth.

Examine the prints critically in good light and select the best ones. Don't use direct sunlight or unusually strong artificial light for the appraisal or you'll find your best prints are too dark when they're seen in a normal setting. Narrow the choice to one or two, paying particular attention to the detail rendering and contrast in the highlights and especially in the shadow areas.

When you have made your choice go back into the darkroom and make another set of three prints on each of the selected papers, again bracketing the exposure around the best test exposure time. Tone these prints slightly in either gold or selenium (see Chapter 12) as you would for archival permanence, so the dark tones are deepened without any obvious change in color. Wash and dry the toned prints as before, and make a new selection. Finally, compare the best untoned prints with the best toned ones and pick the winner, considering every factor including image color. If you're satisfied that the final selection represents your best effort, consider it your standard for the time being.

The purpose of this print test is to determine an effective paper exposure scale, or scale index (SI), based on your personal preference in print density and contrast. It's necessary, therefore, to identify the useful limits of reflection density and contrast represented in the print. You can consider the print minimum density to be ANSI's standard 0.04 over paper B + F, because it's close enough to the absolute white of the paper base to be difficult to measure with precision. The useful Dmax, on the other hand, is debatable. You should select the print tone which seems to represent the first discernible shade lighter than maximum paper black. This is likely to be a difficult decision and, if possible, you should locate several areas on the print which satisfy this condition. Then measure them with your densitometer (in reflectance mode) and record the readings. If there are significant differences (more than about 0.15) in the readings, examine the print again to determine which values are authentic. If the readings are similar, it will be safe to average them to arrive at your personal Dmax. Record the Dmax value; we'll use it in a little while.

It's important to make this judgment on actual print values because if you determine your Dmax from step tablet densities or fogged

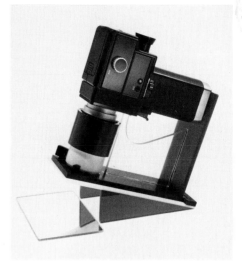

A densitometer conversion unit for the Minolta Spotmeter. Spotmeter densitometers can measure both transmission and reflection densities.

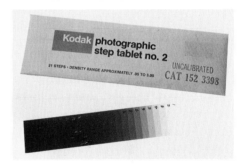

The Kodak step tablet. The steps have been numbered for easy identification.

A Pentax Spotmeter V in its adapter, set up to read reflection densities.

105

paper samples—a traditional recommendation—you're likely to pick an extreme value which will distort your working data. Then, when you use the data for actual printing, you're apt to find your prints coming out with opaque shadows and harsh gradation. If you've tested more than one paper you'll probably find the Dmax values vary somewhat from paper to paper. Toning will increase the Dmax noticeably. The Dmax is also affected by surface texture; glossy surfaces always yield higher Dmax values than matte surfaces do. The important factor here though is not the numerical value of Dmax itself but rather your satisfaction with it as a print tone. If the print looks good, don't worry about the numbers. Rich, luminous shadows are more closely related to contrast and gradation in the dark tones than to high values of density alone.

Now print your step tablet on the selected paper, just as you printed the test negative. If you projected the negative, project the step tablet, but be sure to mask it in the negative carrier with opaque paper or tape so no light can spill around the edges. You can change the magnification if you want to. The step tablet should receive at least 2 or 3 stops more exposure than the negative did (so you'll be sure to have both extremes of tone represented) but provide this added exposure by opening the lens or reducing the magnification rather than by increasing the exposure time significantly. Reciprocity effects will not be very serious unless your normal exposure time is more than doubled (see Chapter 12).

Process the step tablet print just as you did the test prints, and tone it if your standard print was toned. Finally, when the print is dry, read the visible steps with your densitometer in the reflection mode and record the densities, step by step, matching each print density with its corresponding step tablet density, as shown.

Take a worksheet from the Workbook (page 33) and tape it to your drawing board, keeping the graph base line parallel to your T square. Notice that the exposure axis of the graph is marked in log numbers which appear to be in reverse sequence. Although the exposure increases from left to right, the numbers increase from right to left because they are actually the step tablet densities. They can be used on the exposure axis because the steps, when transilluminated by the enlarger light, function as exposing lights for the paper emulsion (Fig. 9-1). The heavy densities transmit only a little light and provide little exposure; the thinner steps transmit a great deal of light and provide much exposure. We can't calibrate the exposure axis in actual units of exposure because we have no way to measure them. However, we do know what the *relative* exposures are because they must be in inverse proportion to the densities that are responsible for them. We *can* measure the densities, so they are convenient for calibration purposes.

Drawing the Paper Curve

Now plot the paper curve. The transmission density values of the step tablet should be indicated along the graph exposure axis, and the reflection density values of the step tablet print are located on the

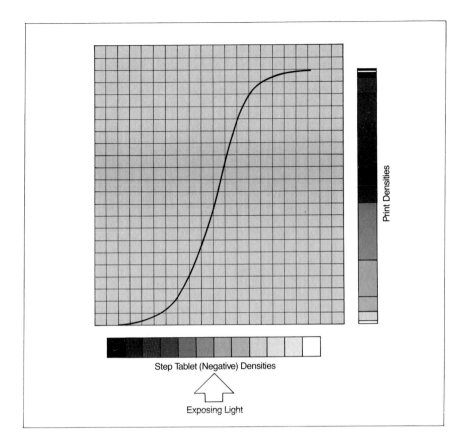

Print Densities

Step Tablet (Negative) Densities

Exposing Light

Figure 9-1. The illuminated step tablet densities serve as exposing lights for the paper test.

vertical density axis of the graph; don't confuse the two. Be sure that you plot corresponding values against each other: tablet step 4 against print step 4, step 6 against print 6; 10 against 10, and so on. If the graph is calibrated correctly and the values are properly matched, the print curve will slope upward from left to right, as in Figure 9-2. Connect your plotted points with a continuous line and average the points, if necessary, to make the line smooth and graceful. It cannot zig-zag erratically or be lumpy or inconsistent.

When the curve has been plotted and evened out with the french curve, locate your personal print Dmin and Dmax values on it. Then drop vertical lines from those points down to the exposure axis of the graph to find your personal paper Scale Index value (Fig. 9-3). If you have tested more than one paper type and drawn curves for each, you'll see the curves have somewhat different shapes and the SI values are not all alike. The curve shape can tell you a lot about image gradation; we'll discuss that later in more detail. The SI number is an indication of effective paper contrast, or grade.

You can check the accuracy of your test results by returning to the original test negative. Measure the densities of the negative which correspond to the print reflection densities you identified as Dmin and Dmax. The negative density range between these extremes should be very similar to the SI value. You can ignore a minor difference but if the difference is more than about 0.15 it would be wise to review your test procedures to find the cause.

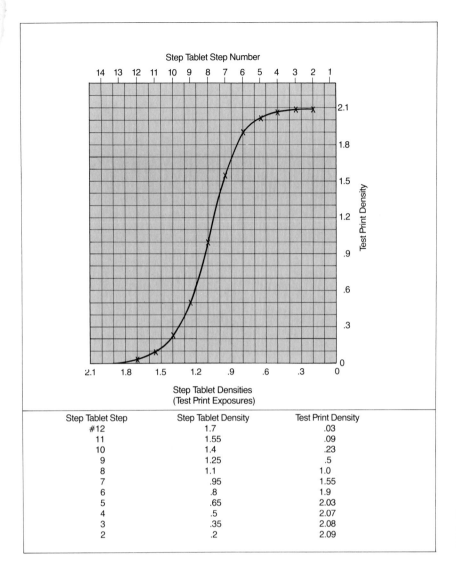

Step Tablet Step	Step Tablet Density	Test Print Density
#12	1.7	.03
11	1.55	.09
10	1.4	.23
9	1.25	.5
8	1.1	1.0
7	.95	1.55
6	.8	1.9
5	.65	2.03
4	.5	2.07
3	.35	2.08
2	.2	2.09

Figure 9-2. If plotted correctly the curve will rise in a graceful s-shape from lower left to upper right.

Troubleshooting

There are several possible causes for error: your curve may be drawn inaccurately, you may have misjudged or misread the negative areas, your print reflection density readings may have been wrong—even a wrinkle in the paper surface or a spot of dust in the reading area can influence the reading. Occasionally the negative image may be a different color from the step tablet image. If one is distinctly more brown than the other it will have a higher effective printing density and contrast because brown is a safelight for paper. This color difference may or may not influence the meter cell, depending on its color sensitivity.

A difference in printing conditions can cause a substantial difference in the ranges too, but if you followed the instructions and printed both test images by projection, or both by contact, you'll avoid this possibility. Printing at different magnifications should not make any appreciable difference, nor should a change in the aperture of the

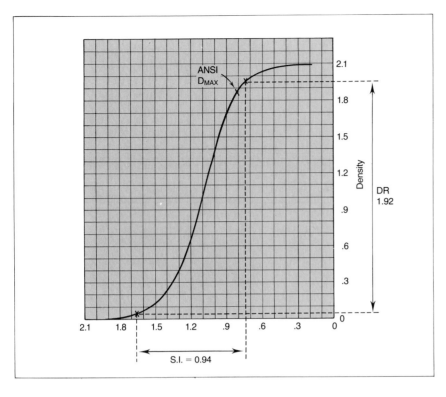

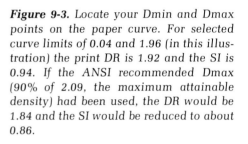

Figure 9-3. Locate your Dmin and Dmax points on the paper curve. For selected curve limits of 0.04 and 1.96 (in this illustration) the print DR is 1.92 and the SI is 0.94. If the ANSI recommended Dmax (90% of 2.09, the maximum attainable density) had been used, the DR would be 1.84 and the SI would be reduced to about 0.86.

enlarging lens, if the lens is clean and of good quality. Exposure time differences, if extreme, can result in contrast differences due to reciprocity failure (see Chapter 12). If the step tablet was not adequately masked during projection it's possible that raw light, leaking around it, may have caused fogging and consequent reduction of image contrast. Safelight fog is another possibility, but this should not be a factor unless one of the test prints was left out in the safelight much longer than the other.

When you have decided on a final value of SI, record it and turn your attention to film testing. This is a more complicated procedure which must be carefully controlled, but it's not difficult once you get used to it. If you proceed logically and stay in control, you can expect good results.

Sheet Film Testing: Exposure

The step tablet again provides known values of exposure but this time you should print it by contact instead of by projection. There is at least one good reason for this: contact printing avoids any possibility of flare. Although it may seem to you that flare is an unavoidable factor which should be included in the test, this is not advisable. At this point we're interested only in the characteristics of the materials—film and developer—themselves. We're not yet ready to consider the effect that camera and lens will have on the final image.

Several other factors must be controlled closely. The test exposure time should be less than 1 second, to avoid reciprocity effects—loss of effective film speed and increased image contrast—as explained at length in Chapter 12. On the other hand, if you use your enlarger timer to control the test exposure, you shouldn't try to use an exposure interval shorter than about 1/10 second. The warm-up and cool-down time of an enlarger bulb will make up a significant portion of the total "on" time of any tungsten-filament bulb, and this will be especially true if your enlarger is equipped with one of the low-voltage, high-intensity bulbs which are now in wide use. Some variation in exposure times is therefore likely. You'll need an electronic timer to get accurate exposures of less than a second; mechanical timers are notoriously unreliable in this speed range.

I recommend exposing the test films in a printing frame on the enlarger baseboard. Raise the enlarger head high enough to illuminate an area about twice as wide as the long dimension of the printing frame and focus the lens as if you were about to make a print. Place the printing frame in the center of the illuminated area and devise a couple of guides which can be used to position the frame precisely in the dark. This is important; if the test films are not exposed to identical light conditions, the test won't be reliable.

Since you'll use the enlarger only as a light source, you may be able to replace the enlarger lens with a shutter-mounted camera lens. Although this will permit accurate control of the brief exposure times, I recommend it only if you don't have an electronic timer. If you have neither a timer nor a suitable shutter, you can use a 35mm camera body, with lens and back removed, as an under-the-lens shutter. Other sorts of cameras can probably be similarly adapted, but I consider these to be desperate measures. If you must use an external shutter of any sort, be sure it doesn't vignette the enlarger light.

Turn out the darkroom lights, turn on the enlarger light with the lens cap on or the shutter closed, and check for light leaks. If you find any, and you probably will, wrap the enlarger head in opaque cloth or use black tape to eliminate as much stray light as you can, particularly if you're planning to leave the light on continuously during the test period and use shutter control of the exposure times. This is less important if you control exposure with a timer because the stray light will be switched with the exposing light and will simply become part of the useful exposure. Regardless of the method chosen be sure there are no patterns or streaks of light, direct or reflected, on the test area.

Most general-purpose films are now fully panchromatic and will respond satisfactorily to all visible colors. It isn't usually necessary, therefore, to filter the enlarger light for your film tests. Although the enlarger light is relatively yellow compared to average daylight, the color difference will not noticeably affect your test results on panchromatic film. Enlarger light is also satisfactory for testing orthochromatic or blue-sensitive films *for use in tungsten illumination*, but if you plan to use these materials in daylight, you should filter the enlarger light to simulate daylight color balance when making the test exposures. Use a blue filter (such as the Wratten #80A) over the enlarger lens.

Tape your step tablet to the printing frame glass so it will remain in position during the test and surround it with strips of heavy paper, such as brown kraft paper from a grocery bag. This will prevent exces-

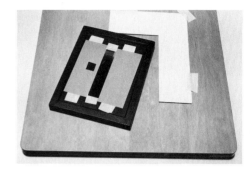

A cardboard guide taped to the enlarger baseboard will help you position the printing frame accurately in the dark.

If you have no alternative you can use a camera shutter to regulate the film test exposure times.

sive exposure of the film area surrounding the test image, reduce light "bleeding" into the image area due to irradiation, and simulate normal, average negative density. If the step tablet is not masked, or if it is masked with opaque material, the test films will not represent normal average exposure and the developer exhaustion rate may be affected unrealistically.

One more recommendation: stick a dime-sized piece of opaque tape on the brown paper mask, close to the step tablet. This will protect a small area of the film from receiving any exposure, and provide you with a reliable B + F reference density in the test negatives.

When everything is ready, turn out the lights, put a sheet of film in the printing frame, emulsion side facing the step tablet, and position the frame against the guides on the enlarger baseboard. Expose for ½ second at about f/16, then process the film in a tray, using your customary procedure and normal developing time for the materials under test. If you haven't yet established a normal time, follow the manufacturer's recommendations.

The developed image should display all but 1 or 2 of the steps against a medium to dark gray background. If *all* the steps are represented in distinct densities, you have given the film too much exposure. If more than 2 steps have failed to show any perceptible density, you'll need to increase the exposure. Make any necessary changes in exposure by adjusting the enlarger height and the lens aperture. Increase the exposure time only if you have no alternative; exposures of more than 1 second risk reciprocity failure.

Underexposing the test films will restrict the useful range of the test, as the top film strip illustrates. The bottom strip has been severely overexposed; it will yield a toeless curve which cannot be analyzed.

Since each step of the step tablet represents a density change of a half-stop from either of its neighbors, the exposure intervals provided by the steps similarly progress in half-stop units. Therefore, if your test negative shows, for example, 6 steps of B + F density, instead of the desired 1 or 2, it indicates the need to increase the test exposure by 4 or 5 half-stops. Correction for overexposure is a little more difficult to estimate but the same principles apply: to shift a given density either way, change the exposure by 1 stop for each 2 steps of shift desired.

Calculate or estimate the necessary exposure correction and make another test. If the second test (using fresh developer, of course) indicates the correction is adequate, you can proceed with the series. If the second test is not satisfactory, it should at least suggest a further correction which will be acceptable. It's probably safe to estimate the correction and proceed with the test series. Expose five films, one after the other, identically, and store them in a light-tight box. Then turn on the lights and prepare your processing chemicals.

Developing the Test Films

I strongly recommend using a one-shot developer and tray-developing sheet films. Tray development, when competently done, is faster and more likely to provide effective agitation than tank development frequently does. Furthermore, the use of a one-shot developer helps to insure uniformity and is quite economical. Unless you have reason to do otherwise, I'd suggest using D-76, diluted 1:1. I think you'll find it to be a remarkably effective and flexible general-purpose developer without any apparent shortcomings. At 1:1 dilution it provides plenty of activity and reserve strength for most films and is inexpensive enough to use lavishly. For higher contrast and reduced developing times it can be used straight; for lower contrast you can work at dilutions of up to about 1:4.

You'll have to standardize on some ratio of developer volume to film area and I suggest you use 4 ounces of the 1:1 solution per 4 × 5 sheet—16 ounces for each sheet of 8 × 10 film. Purists may argue that anything less than a pint per 4 × 5 sheet is risky but in practice 4 ounces has proved to be satisfactory. Make up your own mind; it's a compromise between uniformity of developer strength and chemical economy. Once you've decided on a ratio, though, stick with it.

Prepare a volume of developer sufficient for the 5 test films and bring it to your standard temperature. The actual temperature is not important, within reasonable limits; it's best to pick one that's within a few degrees of the average air temperature in your darkroom. Temperature is an important factor in film development and it must be controlled closely. If there is more than a few degrees difference between the developer and the air temperature, float the developer tray in a much larger tray of water to stabilize the solution temperature. If the room air is warmer than the desired developer temperature, make the water bath a degree or two cooler than the developer. If the room air is cold, make the water bath a degree or two warmer than the desired developer temperature. If you have one, use a stainless steel tray for the developer to maximize heat transfer; plastic trays are such effective insulators that the water bath won't be very effective.

If you're fortunate enough to have an automatic water temperature controller, you can set it for the desired temperature and allow tempered water to flow through the water bath. Check your regulator to see how accurate it is at low flow rates, though; some of them are unreliable when delivering less than one or two gallons per minute.

The stop bath and fixer should also be adjusted to the standard temperature, whatever it is, but will not have to be included in the water bath. A variation of 2 or 3 degrees will not be serious. When the chemicals are ready, place the box of exposed film close by and be sure your interval timer is conveniently located and visible. If the timer has phosphorescent numerals and hands, activate them with a bright light for a minute or two.

Plan your developing times to cover a range from less than half the normal recommended time for the film and developer in use, to more than twice the recommended time. For example, if the normal time is 6 minutes, plan to develop one film for about 2 or 2½ minutes, one at 4, one at 6, one at 9, and one at 15 minutes or more. The very short times are admittedly awkward and difficult to work with but they'll provide useful information. Do your best to make them realistic. Set the timer at the maximum time you've chosen—let's say 15 minutes. Turn off the lights. Now immerse the films in the developer in quick succession, and start the timer. Separate the films as quickly as you can and begin your standard interleaving agitation procedure.

Opposite, top left: Hold the films lightly in one hand, fanning them out like a hand of cards to be sure they're all there. Try to avoid finger contact with the emulsion side. Top right: Place the films flat on the developer surface, and pat them under, one at a time, in quick succession. Be careful to avoid scratching them with your fingernails or with the sharp corners of the other films. Middle left: As soon as all the films are wet you can put both hands in the developer. Herd all the sheets gently into one corner of the tray . . . Middle right: . . . and immediately begin agitating them; raise the stack with one hand and slip the bottom sheet out with the other. Bottom left: Let the stack sink back under the developer and lay the sheet flat on the surface. . . Bottom right: . . . and pat it down gently. Continue this sequence at a leisurely pace until the developing time is up.

The first film, which needs 2½ minutes development, should be removed to the stop bath when the timer reads 12:30. The second film comes out 1½ minutes later, at 11:00. The third should be removed at 9:00, the fourth at 6:00, and the last film stays in for the full time, coming out at 0:00. Fix these numbers in your mind. If you think you'll lose track, you can record the times and incidental instructions on tape and literally talk yourself through the process.

Some photographers like to pre-soak sheet films in plain water for a minute or two before placing them into the developer. This will help prevent the sheets from sticking together when they are first immersed in the developer and will also help prevent uneven development during the first 3 or 4 minutes. It will, however, alter the test results. If you use this technique in the test you must continue to use it in practice. Suit yourself; good results are possible either way.

Although it may seem clumsy and unnecessary to develop the five films together, it's preferable to doing them separately for several reasons. First, the films are subjected to identical conditions of temperature and agitation during the critical early part of their treatment. Second, the test conditions closely approximate the actual working conditions you'll employ later. Third, there's a considerable savings in time. Fourth, developing individual films in small volumes of developer is likely to cause uneven development unless very small trays are used, and the developer exhaustion rate will be disproportionately high for heavily exposed films.

It's been suggested that timing the films would be simplified if they were put into the developer one by one at appropriate intervals and removed together. This should not be done for the obvious reason that the last one or two films will be treated in well-used developer and will get even less development than their short immersion times would normally provide. The longer-developed films, on the other hand, will have the benefit of relatively high volumes of fresh developer for most of their immersion time and will be disproportionately overdeveloped

Five test films as they appear on a light box. The circles drawn on alternate steps indicate the areas to be read with the densitometer. It's usually not necessary to read every step, although it may be useful to do so in the toe region of the curves.

as a result. The best method has proved to be the one first described: put all the films in together and remove them as their respective times expire.

The films can be placed in the stop bath as they come out of the developer and can remain there until the last one is finished. There is no need to identify them at this stage. Then they should be placed in the fixing bath and agitated briefly before the white lights are turned on. Fix, wash, and dry them normally. You should now have a set of images ranging from very low to very high contrast. The lowest contrast image will probably not include any sign of the first two or three steps, and the densest image will probably display a noticeable density on even its thinnest step. This variation is normal and simply demonstrates the effective change in film speed related to development variations.

Drawing the Film Curves

Read the test negative densities and plot them against the original step tablet densities, as has been previously described (page 107). You can use a worksheet, page 44 of the Workbook, or you can use ordinary graph paper. I recommend the inexpensive paper marked 4 squares to the inch, available in pads where stationery and school supplies are sold.

You'll undoubtedly have to do some adjusting to smooth out the curves and make them fit the family. Be careful to average the points and even out any humps or hollows that are inconsistent with the general family contours (Fig. 9-4a and b). Pay particular attention to the spaces between the curves. They must be as uniform and consistent as the curve shapes themselves, especially in the critical toe region. Adjust them as necessary, staying as close as possible to the data points and making the best possible compromises between shape and placement. This sort of adjustment is not cheating; it is, in fact, normal and necessary. In general the errors are minor and as often as not tend to average themselves out. Adjustments of the curves to fit the theoretical norm actually amount to data correction as long as they aren't overdone. Just be certain you don't begin to modify curve contours that are legitimate characteristics of the materials.

You'll have to make one adjustment of the curves which is strictly guesswork: the 10-stop range of the step tablet is not long enough to reach a useful Dmax value on the underdeveloped test negatives and their curves will have to be extended if their data are to be used. This is risky because the shoulder contours of these curves are unpredictable and a relatively slight shift in curve shape will appear to make a considerable difference in the data derived from them. Accept the risk and extend the curves as straight lines for the moment (Fig. 9-5). This will probably require adding an extra sheet of paper to the graph to extend it.

Now proceed with the curve analysis as you have done previously. Find the Dmin line first, then locate Dmax by adding your

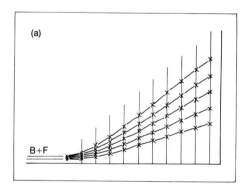

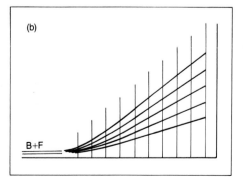

Figure 9-4. *Begin the curve construction by (a) connecting the data points with lightly sketched lines, then (b) smooth them out with your french curve.*

personal value of DR—consider this to be the same as the SI value you found in the paper test—to the Dmin value. Construct the Dmax line, extending it to intersect all the curves. Then find the working data for the system you want to use—SBRs for the incident system, N-numbers for the Zone System.

Data Correction May Be Necessary

If you examine your SBR-(or N-number)-vs.-developing-time chart it may appear that the curve—if extended—will reach, or even cross, the "zero" time line, as in Figure 9-6. This is clearly impossible. Actually, there will probably not be any measurable negative density formed on the film for at least 15 to 30 seconds after its immersion in the developer because it takes that long for the gelatin to become suffused with liquid so the chemical action can begin. If you have treated the film in a preliminary water bath, the appearance of the image will probably be delayed as long or longer, as the water gradually diffuses out of the gelatin and the developer chemicals work their way in. In either case, image formation is delayed for about half a minute. This makes the minimum possible developing time about 30 seconds, not zero seconds, on the chart; and the developing curve, if extended sufficiently, can eventually reach the 30-second line and blend smoothly into it, but it can't cross it to reach zero.

It's safe to assume the developing curve data points are correct within the normal time range and any error introduced by our guesswork extension of the lower curves will be greatest for the lowest developing time. If we assume the development curve will reach the 30-second limit line at some ridiculously high value—theoretically it will reach its limit at an SBR of infinity—we can draw in a new section of the curve which begins near the normal-time data point and blends smoothly into the 30-second line at some point well outside the normal boundaries of the chart (Fig. 9-7). This will have the practical effect of indicating increased developing time for the higher useful values of SBR. In practice this turns out to be appropriate but the actual values will have to be confirmed by field tests.

These seemingly arbitrary alterations in the test data should not be cause for skepticism or alarm. One of the virtues of working with curves, as we've pointed out, is their ability to supply new information between known data points, and to display trends. Although extending a curve beyond its data points is always an uncertain business, some sorts of curves are very predictable and the developing curve is one of them. It can be depended on to become parallel to the vertical and horizontal axes of the graph if the ends are extended far enough. Just be sure that when you extend or correct a curve of this sort, you maintain the character of the curve. Abrupt changes in slope or contour are almost never tolerable.

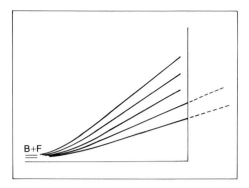

Figure 9-5. The lower curves may not reach a useful density level. Extend them arbitrarily as straight lines; the data can be checked and adjusted later on, if necessary.

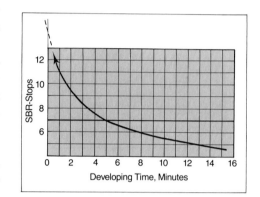

Figure 9-6. The developing time curve may appear to be headed toward zero minutes—impossible.

Troubleshooting the Film Test

Your first few sets of characteristic curves will probably be lumpy and irregular. This will be due partly to inexperience, but it's also likely that you'll discover some errors in the calibration of your step tablet. These too can be corrected by referring to the film curves. If all the curves in a family show a hump or hollow corresponding to the same exposure value or step, it's a pretty good indication that the exposure value is mis-calibrated (Fig. 9-8a). Shift it laterally along the exposure axis of the graph as far as necessary to correct the curve shapes and record the new value. If subsequent curve families are improved by this change, consider it valid and make the calibration change permanent.

Several other problems may arise in making your first tests: the test images may all be too dense so the curves plot without any visible toes (Fig. 9-8b). This is probably due to overexposure of the test films and the necessary correction is obvious. If all the curves appear near the right-hand margin of the graph and fail to reach useful values of DR before they run off the edge (Fig. 9-8c), the text exposure was not sufficient. Increase it. If the B + F level is abnormally high (Fig. 9-8d), your film may have been fogged. This is rare when the test exposures are made in a printing frame, but not uncommon when the tests are made by projection. Check the film to be sure it's fresh, then review the storage conditions to be sure the film hasn't been subjected to excessive heat, humidity, or harmful chemical vapors. There is a slight possibility that the developer may have been improperly mixed or contaminated, perhaps by being stored or measured in unclean containers. The most likely cause, however, is light fog during processing. Check for light leaks in your darkroom and be sure you have turned off your darkroom safelights. You don't need—and shouldn't use—a safelight for film test processing, even if the film is orthochromatic or blue-sensitive.

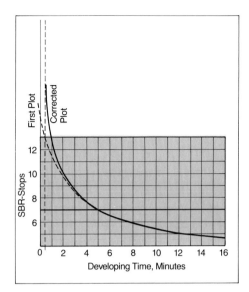

Figure 9-7. *Correct the data arbitrarily by constructing a smooth curve blending into a 30-second minimum time line. Start the new curve at about the 8 or 9-stop SBR level of the chart and keep it flowing gracefully. Although this construction will tend to correct for errors introduced when the film curves were extended, don't take these data too seriously until you've tested them in the field.*

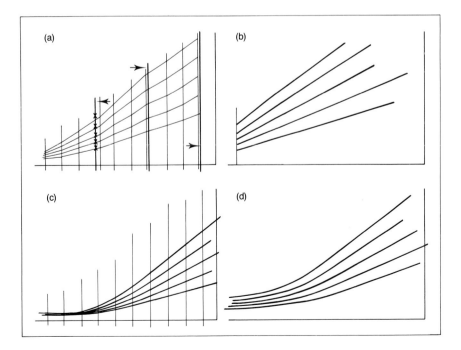

Figure 9-8. *Some curve family problems and what they mean. (a) If all the curves in a family display an unusual hump or hollow at some specific exposure value, you should suspect your step tablet calibration. Move the exposure step left or right until the values produce a smoother curve contour, and proceed. Check this calibration again on your next test to be sure it's valid. (b) If the curve family begins at the far left of the graph and has no useful toes, you've overexposed the test films. (c) If the curves start farther to the right than usual and run off the graph before reaching useful Dmax values, you've underexposed the test films. Don't try to extend them in this case; do the test over. (d) If the curve toes are lengthened and the B + F level is exaggerated, you've probably fogged the test films. You'll get curves like this if you test films in the camera (by photographing the step tablet on a light box). These curves are not usable.*

Occasionally you may encounter a curve which seems properly shaped but which is displaced along the exposure axis so that it crowds or even crosses an adjacent curve. This is probably caused by a variation in the test exposures. If you used a camera shutter it may have misfired for one of the films. If you used an electronic timer, it's more likely that the error resulted from a momentary dimming or brightening of the light due to line voltage fluctuations. In either case, if the curve seems to be compatible with the family in every other respect, it's probably safe to move it back where it belongs. Space it appropriately between its natural neighbors and proceed (Fig. 9-9).

If you are unaccustomed to tray processing it's very likely that you'll get unevenly developed test negatives at first. This will cause the film curves to be irregular and inconsistent in shape; they may even bump into each other, theoretically an impossible situation. To avoid this, practice your film-handling technique until it becomes consistent. Keep your fingers off the emulsion side as much as possible and maintain constant agitation in the developer by extracting the bottom film of the stack, laying it flat on top of the stack, and sloshing developer over it to submerge it. Repeat this sequence continuously, but slowly and gently, for the entire developing period. Don't merely rock the tray. Even working with only one sheet at a time, tray-rocking may not provide adequate agitation, and is likely to cause uneven development. Rotate the films occasionally during development so you'll be touching different corners and edges; repeated or prolonged finger contact in any spot will cause local development variations.

If the curves are reasonably consistent in contour and spacing and if they cover an exposure range of 8 stops or more, you can probably use them for analysis. Check them first, though, to determine whether the working data will be useful. Ideally the curves should represent average gradients of about 0.35 or less to 0.8 or more. If none of the curves show a $\overline{G}$ of less than about 0.45, the test development was overdone; the minimum times should be reduced for the next test, or the developer should be diluted, or the temperature lowered. If none of the curves reach a $\overline{G}$ of at least 0.65, the test development was not sufficient. Increase developing time or developer strength for the next test. In some cases the curves may be rather tightly grouped, displaying very little variation in slope, even though the developing times cover a wide range (Fig. 9-10). This is a characteristic of certain developers and is not an indication of error in your procedures.

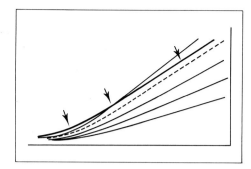

Figure 9-9. *If one of the curves touches or crosses another, and if it is not obviously misshapen, it may simply indicate an exposure variation in the test. If moving it laterally can make it fit into the family, it's probably safe to move it and use it. The heavy solid line curve in this illustration shows the effect of approximately a ½-stop overexposure on that single test film.*

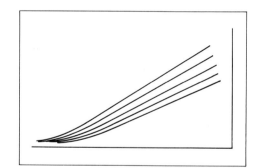

Figure 9-10. *Curves which don't vary much in gradient, but form a consistent family and maintain low to moderate toe density may be accurate and usable. Some highly diluted one-shot developers form curve families of this sort.*

How to Test Rollfilm

Although the preceding discussion has assumed the use of sheet film, it's possible to test rollfilm by cutting a roll into five or more pieces and handling them as if they were sheets. It's even possible to work this way with 35mm stock if you want to, but it complicates development. Rollfilm and 35mm film is usually developed in small tanks with intermittent agitation; tray development, though probably the most practical method for handling small pieces of film, will give unrealistic development data for tank use.

You have at least two options: you can develop the test pieces in a tray, analyze the negatives, derive working curves and adjust them by field tests; or you can make the test exposures on roll or 35mm films without cutting them, then develop in a tank, more or less as usual. This last procedure should produce usable working charts directly but will require a different test exposure procedure.

Rollfilm Test Exposure. Photographing the step tablet on a light box has been suggested, but I can't recommend in-camera testing of any sort; there's too much likelihood of serious flare. You'll get more reliable results if you rig up a makeshift contact printer, like the one shown, and use it under your enlarger. To make a printer for 35mm film testing, cut two short slits, about 1½ inches long and about 6 inches apart, in the top of a cardboard box and cover the space between the slits with a strip of foam plastic about 2 inches wide and ⅛ inch thick. Cover the foam pad with a piece of black paper or cloth. Hinge a piece of glass or clear plastic, about 4 inches × 8 inches, to the box top, with a strip of tape along one edge so it can be dropped down to cover the pad. Insert the ends of a strip of scrap 35mm film into the two slits, so the ends are inside the box, and flatten the film strip out on the paper-covered pad. Then tape your step tablet to the underside of the glass so it will cover the film, emulsion down, when the glass is lowered. Mask the step tablet with black paper or black tape on all sides, extending the mask material far enough to cover the box slits when the glass is pressed down against the foam pad.

A makeshift contact printer for exposing roll film.

For 120 rollfilm tests, cut the slits in the box top about 2½ inches long and about 4 inches apart. Then cut a step tablet in half and tape the halves, side by side, on the underside of the hinged glass.

To use the print box, turn out the lights, remove the box cover, and thread the end of a roll of film up through one of the slits, across the foam pad—emulsion up—and down through the other slit. Replace the cover on the box. Press the glass plate, bearing the step tablet, down on the film and make the exposure under the enlarger, as usual. To advance the film for the next exposure, raise the glass plate, grasp the film close to the first slit (punch a small hole in it, with scissors or a paper punch, to mark the end of the exposed area), and pull it across the foam pad, tucking the slack down the second slit into the box. Expose as before and repeat until the film is used up. Then cut the film strip loose, pull it out of the box, and load it onto your tank reel. Store it in an extra tank or a light-tight drawer while you prepare the chemicals.

Developing Rollfilm. You can use almost any rollfilm tank for selective development but it's easiest with a stainless steel tank, such as those made by Nikor, Kindermann, or Brooks. Prepare the chemicals as previously described, fill the tank with developer, and set it in a large water bath at the appropriate temperature. Fill a tray with stop bath to a convenient depth and provide a tray of fixing bath. Lay out a pair of old scissors where you can find them in the dark, activate your timer numerals so you can see them clearly (or get your prerecorded timing tape ready to run) and turn out the lights. Equip the loaded film reel with a lifter if you have one. Start the timer. Immerse the reel in the open tank of developer and alternately rotate and lift the reel out of the

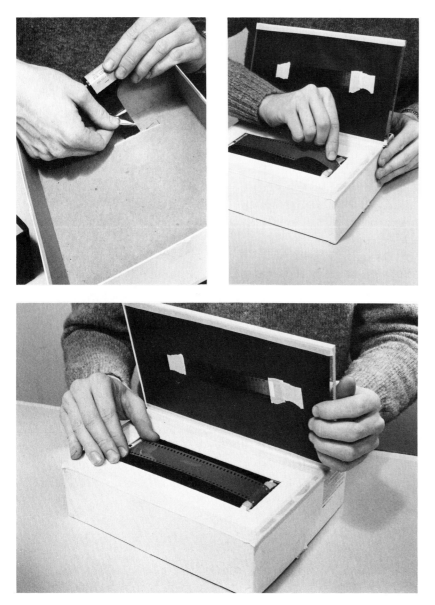

Left: Insert the tongue of the film through the slit in the box cover, from the inside, so the emulsion side will be exposed as the film strip lies on the pad. Right: Close the box and turn out the lights. Pull enough film out through the first slit so that you can tuck the exposed leader through the second slit.

Straighten the unexposed film out and center it on the pad. Make the exposure by lowering the hinged glass into firm contact with the film and punching the timer button. After each exposure, raise the glass, grasp the film near the supply end, as shown here, pull it across to the other slit, mark it with a punch, and tuck the slack into the box. When all the film has been exposed, cut it loose and load it into your tank.

solution for about 15 seconds, rapping it on the edge of the tank once or twice to dislodge any air-bells. Then let it rest for 15 seconds. Thereafter, rotate and lift the reel out of the tank and replace it quickly once every 30 seconds throughout the developing time.

About 15 seconds before the first developing time interval is up, remove the reel from the tank, locate the first punch mark or (if you didn't mark the exposed areas) unroll about 12 inches of 35mm film—about 7 inches of 120 rollfilm—and snip it off with the scissors, letting it fall into the stop bath tray as the time expires. Agitate it with one hand as you use the other to return the reel to the tank to continue the development. Let the cut-off strip rest in the stop bath, face down, so the edges won't curl up out of the liquid. Follow this procedure as each time interval expires, but after the first time (if the film is not marked) cut off only about 8-inch or 10-inch pieces of 35mm film—4 inches or 5 inches of 120 rollfilm. You won't need to worry about cutting the frames in two; as long as you cut off a piece of film longer than a single test frame, you're bound to get all the step tablet even if it isn't all

in one piece. Be sure your first cut includes enough extra film to take care of the unused leader. The leader may be as much as 4 or 5 inches long. When all the strips have been developed and rinsed in the stop bath, fix, wash, and dry them as usual, and proceed with their analysis.

Although there are quite a few photographers who claim to use the Zone System with 35mm film, neither the Zone System nor any other similar system is truly compatible with rollfilms of any size. Real control of the image depends on matching each film exposure with a specific degree of development to produce a negative of optimum quality. It's true this can be done with rollfilm if you're willing to commit an entire roll to each subject condition and develop it appropriately, but this is both awkward and wasteful in practice. The practical alternative is to expose and develop each roll to favor the majority of subject types represented and salvage the abnormal negatives by printing them on compensating contrast grades of paper.

This is not to say that sensitometry is of no value to photographers who work with 35mm. It deals with principles common to all formats, and understanding the principles will improve your efficiency with any camera. Practical application of the derived data is more appropriate for sheet film than rollfilm, however, because sheet film facilitates individual control of negative image quality and rollfilm doesn't. It's as simple as that.

Top left: Start development by lowering the loaded reel into the open tank, full of developer, in the dark. Agitate by lifting the reel out of the developer and replacing it once every 30 seconds (or use your own method). When the first time interval is up, remove the reel. Top right: Locate the first punch mark or pull enough film off the reel to be sure you've got one full test exposure . . . Bottom left: . . . and snip it off with scissors, letting it fall into a convenient tray of stop bath. Bottom right: Quickly tuck the free film end back onto the reel and replace the reel in the developer with one hand while you agitate the cut piece in the stop bath with the other. Let the films accumulate in the stop bath. If they are agitated for 15 seconds or so when first immersed in the bath, they'll be safe until the process is over. You don't have to worry about marking them for identification; the densitometer will sort them out for you.

CHAPTER
10

Beyond the Zone System: The Wonder Wheel

Once you get the hang of the Zone System, it's easy to use and it works. Beginners frequently have trouble, though, for several reasons. Most commonly, in my experience, they have difficulty visualizing the subject values as they should appear in print form. This is partly due to the fact that they don't have a clear idea of what tones of gray the zone values represent. They're also influenced by local contrasts and fail to judge the subject as a whole. Because of these problems, they may try to assign zone values unrealistically, asking the system to provide print value relationships which are simply not possible. These difficulties can be minimized if the print zone values can be compared visually, instead of mentally, with the subject luminance values.

Zone System Weaknesses and Attempts at Correction

Minor White, in *The New Zone System Manual*, suggests making a *zone ruler* for this purpose, and this is certainly a step in the right direction. Another aid, mentioned previously, is a zone scale of grays affixed to the meter dial. (See photo on page 75.) This is not particularly useful for visual comparison with the subject values, but it does provide direct reference to their luminance measurements. Neither of these devices is ideal. The zone ruler points up the differences between subject value relationships and print values, but doesn't provide any corrective information; it merely warns you that you're about to get into trouble without suggesting any way out of it. The meter scale works admirably for determining N-numbers but is too tiny to be a useful visual guide and merely symbolizes print tones without accurately representing them.

Even if these problems could be overcome, the Zone System would still suffer from one practical limitation: the N-numbers, and therefore exposure and development information, must be determined from measurements of two specific subject luminance values. Usually these values are Zones III and VII but they can be any other pair you have determined by test. You do not, however, have complete freedom of choice. If your data are based on III and VII, you have to measure III and VII if you want accurate information. In practice this is a handicap. Your subject may not contain any luminances that correspond to these zones, or you may decide you'd rather deal with another pair of zones. In either case you have to guess at some correction because your working data are reliable only for the test conditions—whatever they were.

It would be preferable to have working access to all the zones. In certain situations some internal contrast is more important than the mere inclusion of "good" shadow detail. Still greater refinement of the process would be possible if the data included working information for specific materials. The gradation characteristics of Super-XX film are quite different from those of Tri-X, for example, and Azo paper will produce highlight tonality which can't be duplicated on, say, Ilford Multigrade. Although these considerations can be included in the Zone System, they're more effective if coupled with a system which permits *visual* comparison of subject luminances with print values.

Zakia and Dowdell expanded the conventional Zone System concept to include this sort of visual reference when they devised their "Zone Systemizer." This ingenious little calculator displayed for the first time, the changing relationships of subject luminances and print values, and included provision for exposure compensation. It continues to provide the most advanced and flexible method for applying the Zone System; however, it still leaves room for improvement. It doesn't allow complete freedom of zone choice, for example, and its gray scale is only a general indication of print tone distribution and not tailored to the characteristics of any specific materials. Finally, it still clings to the concept of zones.

Although traditionalists may insist the zone concept is inseparable from the system and that visualization is impossible without it, this is not necessarily true. Certainly for people who are familiar with the Zone System and who are comfortable with their mental picture of the zone grays, the concept is useful and perhaps even indispensable. There is ample evidence in the work of Adams, White, and many others, to confirm the practicality of the concept when it is understood and used intelligently.

The major value of the zones, however, is that they provide a simple and logical means of remembering what the print grays look like. As long as the system is based on the idea of *mental* comparison between subject and print values, the simplified gray scale represented by the 7 zones is adequate. We are happy to trade subtlety of gradation for ease of remembrance. But when a *visual* comparison is possible, and memory is not a factor, it would seem logical to use more than 7 grays. Since both subject and print exhibit continuous unstepped gradation from light to dark, it would appear that the ideal reference scale should be similarly unstepped. There are two objections to this, however: unstepped scales are extremely difficult to print accurately and

they are too ambiguous to use easily for comparison or selection of specific values. The best compromise, then, is probably a many-stepped scale.

Why the Zones May Be Misleading

The 7 grays which are customarily identified as zones are the print values that result when a 7-stop subject is photographed. As has been pointed out, the print image is a distortion of the subject; both highlight and shadow values are compressed, or reduced in contrast, and the mid-tones are expanded, or increased in contrast. Although we are aware of this distortion, and it is technically unavoidable, it is not ideal. The subject values are evenly spaced and if the print is to be an accurate representation of the subject the print grays *should* be evenly spaced too.

Zone System users have worked around this tonal distortion to achieve the print values they want—in the shadows particularly—by

"Porch Railing" by Howard Bond. Exposure and development were calculated from empirically derived data in the traditional Zone System manner. Zones III and VI were metered; Royal Pan film was developed in HC-110B for 8′ 45″ (considered to be N + 2) and the print was made on Ilfobrom #3, developed in Dektol. Courtesy of the photographer.

fudging their zone assignments. We know from experience, for example, that Zone II in the subject is a more detailed and luminous value than Zone II in the print. To simulate that appearance in the print we may assign the Zone II luminance reading to Zone III or even IV. In other words, we deliberately distort the zone placement to achieve a visualized print value. This procedure becomes intuitive with experience, but it can also be formalized if a reference gray scale is provided which includes the necessary compensation. This has to be the exact opposite of the zone ruler gray scale, which merely displays the print value distortion as it normally occurs.

Engineers frequently design control devices that involve feedback. For example, the speed of a lawnmower engine can be regulated by a centrifugal governor which is operated by the engine itself. When the engine exceeds a predetermined speed, the governor reduces the throttle setting and causes the engine to slow down. When the engine drops below a certain speed, the governor increases the throttle setting causing the engine to speed up. When connected in this manner, the engine circuit is said to have "negative feedback" and the circuit is self-regulating. If the governor is connected backwards, a speed increase will result in greater gas flow and the engine will run faster, causing still more gas flow and greater speed until the engine destroys itself. This is called "positive feedback"—a condition in which errors tend to magnify themselves.

The conventional zone ruler, used as a reference for determining zone placement, introduces positive feedback into the system. If the distortion inherent in the ruler image is fed back into the new film exposure, the resulting print image is doubly distorted. What is needed is a reference scale which reverses the normal print tone distortion. When this information is fed back into the new film exposure, the process distortion will be cancelled and the print values will emerge as uniformly spaced grays. Of course, this will not alter the fact that the process distorts, but it will help you cope with the distortion and control the ultimate print values more accurately than is usually possible.

The Wonder Wheel

Combining these desirable features into a single device has led to the development of a dial calculator which one of my students, a few years ago, named the "Wonder Wheel." It employs a 21-step "fan" of grays, consisting of actual print values, which can be used to make direct visual comparisons with subject luminance values. The concept of zones is unnecessary and is not included in the design. Any pair of luminance values can be used to determine camera settings, since there are no N-numbers involved, and the relative tonality of all subject luminance values is displayed. Exposure compensation is included in the fan design and development information is indicated by the position of the fan, once the luminance values are selected. Finally, the fan slides are derived from specific combinations of film, developer, and paper type so that subtleties of gradation, unique to each combination of materials, can be considered and compared. The Wonder Wheel

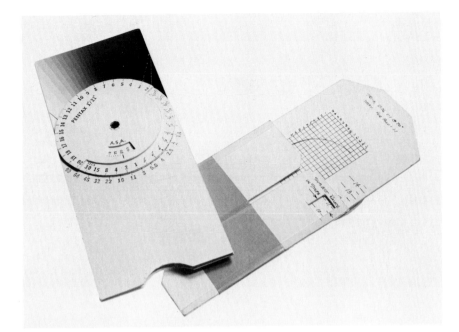

Wonder Wheel calculators, front and rear.

provides a useful *technical* guide for producing perfect prints. The weak link in the process is the photographer—you.

The Wonder Wheel included in the Workbook is not as precise as one you can make yourself. It should be functional, though, and it will demonstrate the principles from which the original design evolved. You can check the accuracy of this copy of the device by reading the densities of the fan segments with your reflection densitometer. Zero the instrument on the white area outside the fan. The fan densities should begin at about 0.04 and increase in increments of approximately 0.08. The Dmax should be 1.7 or more. If your fan densities are close to these values your Wonder Wheel should be useful as is. If not, see Chapter 11 for instructions for making your own slides.

Calibrating the Wheel. Cut out the Wonder Wheel, on the back cover of the Workbook, and assemble it as instructed. The wheel is complete except for the luminance values and your personal developing data. Calibrate it to correspond with your meter, as follows. Set both the Wonder Wheel and the meter on the same ASA number—for example, 100. Set both dials to read the same camera settings, for example, 1/30 second at f/8. Note the luminance value indicated by the normal pointer on the meter calculator dial; if you are using a CdS Luna-Pro, the number is 16.

The central straight line on the fan gray scale corresponds to the meter normal pointer. It will point to a blank space on the calculator dial. Mark 16—or the number your meter displays—in the indicated space. Now complete the scale calibration by marking successive spaces in a clockwise direction with descending numbers—15, 14, 13, 12, etc. Similarly, mark the spaces counterclockwise from the normal line with ascending numbers, 17, 18, 19, 20, etc. Again, these numbers are correct for the CdS Luna-Pro. If you have a different meter, use the numbers from its scale; any reflectance meter can be used with the Wonder Wheel.

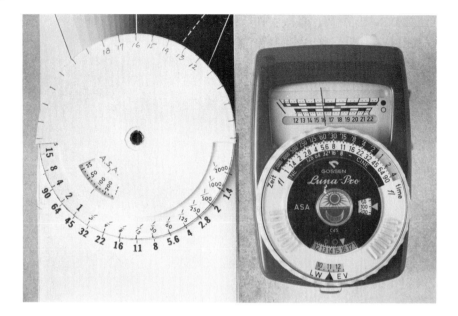

Set both meter and Wonder Wheel dials on ASA 100 and similar camera settings, as shown here. Then mark the Wonder Wheel luminance scale, opposite the fan center line, with the luminance value indicated on the meter dial. Complete the calibration with lower values of luminance to the right and higher values to the left of the center line.

Using the Wonder Wheel. Using the wheel is very simple. Follow this procedure until you are familiar with its operation:

Step 1. Set the ASA film speed (as rated by the manufacturer) into the ASA window of the calculator dial and tape the two discs of the dial together to prevent slippage.

Step 2. Select your subject area and inspect it critically to determine the value relationships you want to record. Identify the subject areas that you want to appear in the print as accent black and white; this is very important.

Step 3. Select two subject areas, one light value and one dark, which you most want to control. They can be any two values but it's best if they are quite different from each other.

Step 4. Select from the fan a stripe of gray that represents the print value you want the light subject area to turn into. Measure the luminance of the light subject area and set that luminance value over the selected fan stripe by turning the dial.

Step 5. Select a dark gray stripe representing your desired print value for the dark area of the subject; meter the luminance and place the value over the dark stripe. You'll probably have to slip the slide in or out of the sleeve and turn the calculator dial to do this without moving the light value off its selected stripe.

Step 6. When both values are properly matched with their respective stripes, check several other subject areas to see if their luminance values fall on stripes of suitable gray tone. Check the accent extremes of black and white as you perceive them in the subject to be sure they fall on or outside the limits of the fan gray scale. If they fall within the fan area they will be recorded as toned or textured values.

Step 7. If any subject luminance value is matched with an inap-

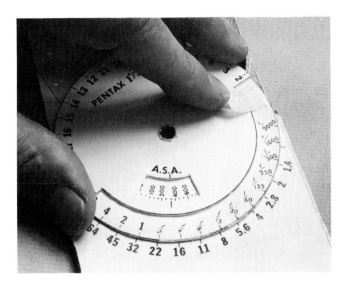

High Value=15   Accent Black
Low Value=9

No Measurable
Accent White

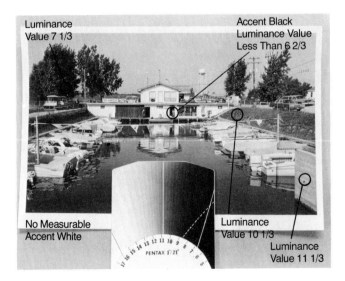
Luminance
Value 7 1/3

Accent Black
Luminance Value
Less Than 6 2/3

No Measurable
Accent White

Luminance
Value 10 1/3

Luminance
Value 11 1/3

Top left: Set the ASA speed and tape the dials together (Step 1).

Top right: Identify the accents of black and white if they exist in the subject. In this case, the open doorway can represent accent black, but there are no measurable accent whites present; all the large white areas should be slightly toned or textured. The selected light and dark areas measure 15 and 9 respectively (Step 3).

Middle left: Set luminance value 15 on its appropriate near-white fan stripe (Step 4).

Middle right: Set luminance value 9 on its appropriate dark gray fan stripe, adjusting the slide as necessary to keep 15 placed properly (Step 5).

Bottom left: Check some other subject luminance values to see if they fall on suitable tones of gray on the fan. Be sure accent black falls outside the boundary line (Step 6).

propriate gray stripe on the fan, review your visualization to see if you can arrive at a satisfactory compromise. When most of the subject luminance values fall on desirable print tones, proceed with the exposure correction.

Step 8. The fan is marked with two lines, one solid and one dotted. Note the luminance value on the calculator dial which falls over the dotted line (a), then carefully turn the dial to position that reading—whatever it was—over the solid line (b). This will move the luminance values away from their respective grays; don't worry about it—they have accomplished their purpose by establishing the position of the fan slide. Although this exposure correction may seem extreme, it is only because it is being done on a mid-value instead of the more usual Dmin. The actual exposure adjustment is considerably less drastic than it may appear and is correct for Dmin.

Step 9. Select a lens opening and shutter speed combination and make the exposure.

Step 10. Turn the Wonder Wheel over and read the subject range in the window marked SBR. Mark the film holder with the SBR for later identification.

Step 11. Back in the darkroom, develop as indicated on the chart.

Notice that you use your exposure meter only for taking the luminance readings. The meter's calculator is not involved. This is necessary because the meter is set up to work only with subjects of normal range; the sliding fan feature of the Wonder Wheel permits it to function with subjects of any reasonable range.

If your experience with the Wonder Wheel is typical, you'll find the actual operation quite easy after the first few trials. You'll probably also get some rather funny-looking negatives at first. Print them anyway, then look them over carefully. You'll probably find the process has recorded your selected areas just about the way you asked it to but that other areas of the print simply don't look right. This is probably a problem of visualization. You'll have to pay more attention to the selection of the fan grays and correlate them more closely with the luminance values of the subject. This approach to image control is more precise than the usual Zone System procedure and it allows you to make more sophisticated mistakes than you're probably accustomed to. It's a little like driving a Ferrari after you've been used to commuting in an old station wagon; the first few times out you're bound to over-control and scare yourself a little. Don't give up, though. You'll get used to using the wheel and learn to appreciate the flexibility and control it gives you.

Data corrections are made as described in previous chapters with one exception: consistent overexposure or underexposure should be compensated for by changing the ASA setting on the calculator dial. Contrast problems are corrected by altering the developing chart curve. Pay particular attention to process details if you want to make best use of the Wonder Wheel. Careless control of developer variables, in particular, will tend to nullify its advantages.

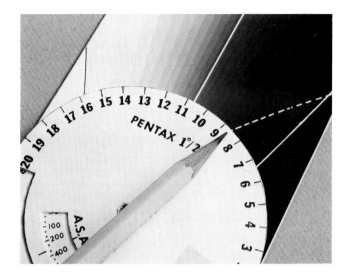

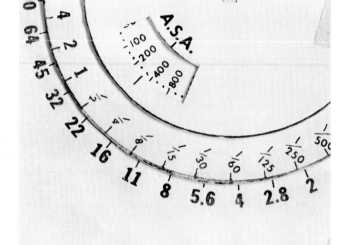

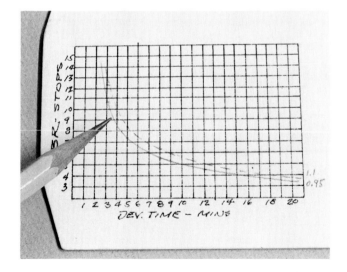

Top left: Identify the luminance value that falls over the broken line on the fan. . . (Step 8a).

Top right: . . . and turn the dial so that luminance value is repositioned to fall over the central solid line. This adjustment takes care of the necessary exposure compensation (Step 8b).

Middle left: Select the camera settings (Step 9).

Middle right: Find the SBR in the window on the back of the Wonder Wheel and mark the film holder (or record the SBR and the holder number) for later references (Step 10).

Bottom left: Back in the darkroom, develop as indicated on the chart (Step 11).

How to Make Your Own Wonder Wheel Slides

You should understand that the Wonder Wheel isn't intended to protect you from gross errors in exposure and development calculation. It is intended to help you sharpen your perception, assist you in appraising your subject matter, and suggest alternative ways of interpreting it. Of course the wheel, like any tool, will work only when you learn how to handle it and, since it's a fairly sophisticated device, you'll be able to use it best if you understand how it works and what it can do.

What the "Fan" Displays

The 21-step fan of grays is the the Wonder Wheel's unique feature. The shape and width of the individual gray segments, their relationship to each other and to the subject luminance values on the calculator dial, provide an informative visual indication of the tone reproduction cycle of the specific materials—the film, film developer, paper, and print finishing treatment—used to make the original test. The fan, in other words, describes the tone distortion that will occur between film exposure and print presentation. It also indicates the print tones which will result from any subject values under any conditions of exposure and development.

There are, of course, many possible pairings of film, developer, and paper; and each combination will produce results that vary, at least slightly, from the others. If these differences don't seem significant to you, you probably don't need the wheel. The Zone System, the Incident System, or just average metering will probably be satisfactory.

On the other hand, you may be the sort of process nut who revels in complication for its own sake. If that's the case—and there's nothing immoral about it—you'll probably not only enjoy the wheel but may also want to equip yourself with fan slides for every possible combination of variables. If you do, however, you'll need a large briefcase to carry them around in.

Most wheel users will steer a compromise course. It's convenient to have slides for the most frequently used materials and for a few of the unusual ones, perhaps four or five in all. Practically speaking, you'll find it difficult to justify more because the processes can't be controlled closely enough to exploit the subtle differences between most common materials. You won't find any major differences between the gradation characteristics of Plus-X and Royal Pan sheet film, for example, and if you consider the image itself, apart from how it was formed, one developer is much like another—with the possible exception of compensating types.

Papers are another matter, but fine printers are fussy about print color, surface, and tonal range, and won't use just any paper. You'll probably be able to work with the paper you like best without limiting your options for gradation control, especially if you're willing to consider testing more than just the normal contrast grade.

Gradation Characteristics of Films and Papers

The gradation potential of a film is indicated by its characteristic curves. Among common film types the differences are subtle, but long-toe curves tend to reduce shadow contrast and emphasize highlight contrast; short-toe curves are likely to give excellent low-value separation but may leave the highlights a little dull. Medium-toe films represent a compromise between these extremes. In general, a curve that exhibits a shoulder tendency within the normal usable subject range will reduce highlight contrast, perhaps to an unpleasant degree. Fortunately, sheet films of this sort are rare. In Figure 11-1 these curve types are diagrammed and the 7-stop range of a normal subject is shown translated into negative densities. Their characteristic distortion of tone is evident in the uneven spacing of the negative densities.

Papers have a similar effect on gradation but the distortion is much more severe for two reasons: first, the contrast of paper emulsions is much higher than that of most films and the toe and shoulder contours are much more drastic; second, most of the paper curve must be used to achieve a full range of print tones and that means almost all of the toe and at least some of the curve shoulder are involved.

It's more difficult to generalize about paper curve shapes because papers seem to be less consistent in their characteristics than films are. Perhaps they are less precisely controlled during manufacture, or perhaps they are more affected by age and storage conditions. There are examples of long-, medium-, and short-toe papers, however, and also differences in shoulder contour. Figure 11-2 diagrams some representative types and shows the translation of uniform increments of exposure into obviously non-uniform increments of density in the print. These distorted patterns of print tone are apparently the basis for the zone rulers recommended by White, Zakia, and Lorenz.

In practice, film and paper distortions frequently compound each

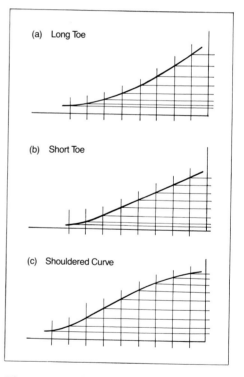

Figure 11-1. *The shape of the film curve is an indication of negative gradation. (a) Long-toe film curves tend to reduce deep shadow contrast and emphasize highlight contrast. (b) Short-toe films tend to separate deep shadow tones well. Midtones and highlights are rendered in more or less uniform gradation. (c) Shouldered curves tend to reduce highlight separation.*

134

other. Figure 11-3a shows how the negative formed by a medium-toe film curve affects a medium-toe paper to form a print image. Compare this with the print gradation resulting from pairing a long-toe film with a short-toe, long-shoulder paper (Fig. 11-3b) and a short-toe film with a long-toe paper (Fig. 11-3c). The major differences are in the mid-range, where print gradation shifts are most apparent. This suggests that a given subject, photographed with different combinations of materials, can be made to yield a variety of subtly different prints. If this possibility intrigues you, you'll appreciate the wheel. It's the only device currently available which permits you to predict and effect this sort of control.

See Section 3 (pages 59-72) of the Workbook for patterns and instructions for constructing your own Wonder Wheel. If you want to manufacture your own slides you'll have to have some way of measuring reflection densities. If you've constructed the spotmeter adapter, described in the appendix and the Workbook, you're well-equipped. Unfortunately, I can't suggest any inexpensive alternative.

Finding the Fan Data

The calculations are all based on characteristic curves of the selected materials. For this illustration let's again use Tri-X sheet film, tray-developed in D-76 1:1, with constant agitation at 20°C. We'll assume the prints are to be made on a medium-toe paper (such as

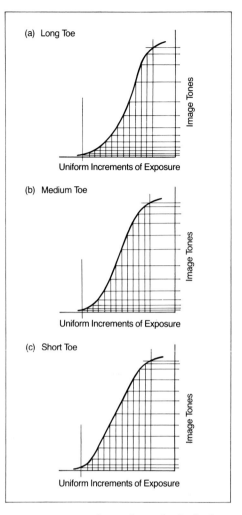

Figure 11-2. Three hypothetical—but representative—paper curves showing differences in print image gradation due to curve shape.

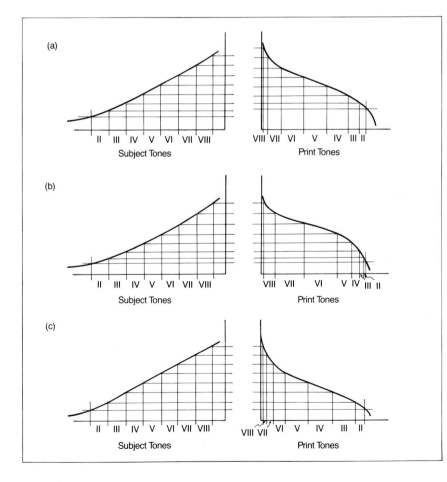

Figure 11-3. In practice the film and paper characteristics combine to produce tonal distortion in the print image. To see how various combinations of materials affect gradation, compare the evenly spaced subject tones with their print counterparts. Tones are labelled with zone numbers for identification. (a) Medium-toe film; medium-toe paper. (b) Long-toe film; short-toe, long-shoulder paper. (c) Short-toe film; long-toe paper. Obviously, many combinations are possible.

Polycontrast, unfiltered). Because the print is the final step in the process, and by far the most important one, we'll begin with the reflection density scale of the paper.

Figure 11-4 shows a Polycontrast-type paper curve (stylized and simplified for convenience) and indicates the limits I would select as appropriate for my own work. You should, of course, plot your own paper curves, as outlined in Chapter 9. Notice that my useful Dmax is greater than the ANSI specification (remember the 90% of absolute Dmax that ANSI considers normal?) because I prefer print blacks as rich as I can get them without losing shadow separation. The paper curve shape has a rather abrupt shoulder, which retains adequate shadow contrast at near maximum density. If the curve shoulder was more gradual I'd pick a lower limit to avoid loss of shadow detail.

Because we consider a 7-stop subject range normal, and because 7 stops equals a log range of 2.1—21 steps of 0.1 each—we'll divide the print density range into 21 equal steps so the individual segments will relate to specific $1/3$-stop increments of the normal SBR. These density divisions won't necessarily equal 0.1 each; they'll be $1/21$ of whatever the selected DR is. In this instance, the total useful range of the paper, as I've determined it, is about 1.7, so the individual steps will span about 0.08 each.

The reason for dividing the print range into even increments instead of the grossly distorted spaces that actually occur, is to *idealize* the print. If the process was perfect and no tone distortion occurred at either the negative or print stage, the subject luminance increments—which *are* uniform—would appear in the print as similarly uniform increments of reflection density. It doesn't actually work this way, but considering the neat full-stop divisions of the subject luminance range that the meter presents, it's easy to forget that the print scale won't be equally neat and uniform.

You have two options: you can work with the uniform subject divisions if you can visualize the print effects and compensate for them by juggling zone assignments (this is what experienced Zone System users do when they make their intuitive adjustments), or you can assume the *print* density divisions should be uniform and work with varied increments of *subject* tone. This is what the Wonder Wheel does. In practice there is no difference in the final print if the systems are used with equal effectiveness; it's merely a difference in concept and approach. The Zone System requires experience and intuition and supplies relatively limited data; the wheel displays the necessary technical information in objective form and encourages visual (instead of mental) solution of the problems.

Reversing the Tone Cycle

Assuming the print divisions should be uniform, the first step in the construction is to project these even divisions back through the curve to the print exposure scale to see what units of exposure are necessary to produce them. This has been done in Figure 11-5, which shows the 21 steps contained within the print SI of 1.0. If we assume

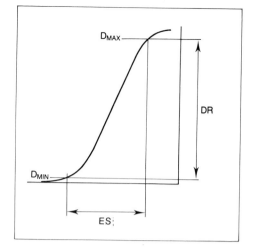

Figure 11-4. *A stylized paper curve with characteristics which suggest Kodak Polycontrast used without a filter. Dmax has been chosen to use as much of the curve length as possible without encountering the shoulder.*

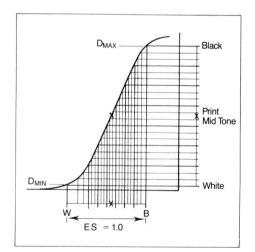

Figure 11-5. *Here 21 uniform increments of print density are traced backwards through the curve to find their corresponding values of print exposure. Print midtone is marked with a small x.*

the paper SI to be identical to the negative DR (see page 108) we can transfer the 21 SI divisions to the film DR where they will represent 21 uneven increments of negative density. Notice that the middle density of the print DR has been marked with a small x. We'll refer to it later.

At this point you can make another personal decision about the conditions of use; you don't necessarily have to position the negative DR at the usual place on the density axis. Normally the negative Dmin will fall at 0.1 over B + F because that produces the thinnest negative which is usually considered to yield satisfactory shadow density and detail. In fact, though, the Dmin can be selected to suit your preference. If you like the effect of murky darks and accented highlights, pick a Dmin of, say, 0.05 or even less. If you like well-detailed shadows and don't mind extended printing times, set your Dmin level at 0.2 or even 0.3. Make this decision thoughtfully. The limit you select will control the exposure of your films and influence print gradation. In this example we'll use the conventional Dmin value of 0.1.

Position the low limit of the 21-step DR at your selected point (0.1 over B + F) on one of the film curves and project each division over to the curve and down to the film exposure axis, using your T square and triangle for accuracy (see Chapter 5). Here the spacing of the steps is obviously abnormal. Follow this procedure for each curve in turn, using the same 21-step negative values for each. Be sure to work from the appropriate B + F level for each curve when locating the Dmins. When all the SBRs have been determined, label each with its range in stops, as shown in Figure 11-6.

Untitled photograph by Kim Hill. Using his Wonder Wheel, Kim metered the white of the boat dock and the darkest shadows under the boat to establish useful tonal extremes, then checked the shadow area inside the boat for proper value rendering. He found the SBR to be 7½ stops. Other data unavailable. Photograph courtesy of the photographer.

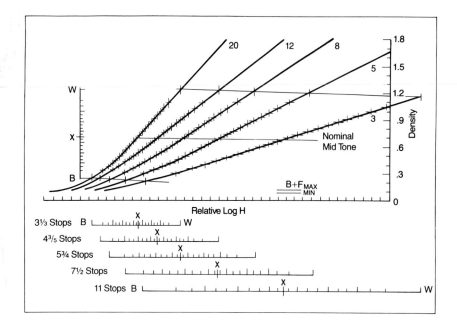

Figure 11-6. Here negative densities corresponding to the uneven increments of print exposure found in Figure 11-5 are traced back through the film curves to find their corresponding values of subject luminance. The mid-point of the print DR is indicated with a small x. Notice that the x is not in the center of any of the negative or subject ranges, although it remains the nominal mid-point.

Arranging the SBRs

It's apparent that all five SBRs are distorted, but there are discernible differences. These differences are more apparent when we arrange the SBRs on a common central axis (representing print middle density) and connect the points to create a fan (Fig. 11-7). Shading the stripes to increase in density from left to right will produce a crude representation of uniformly increasing print densities, non-uniformly spaced (Fig. 11-8). This rudimentary fan can be used for visualizing the

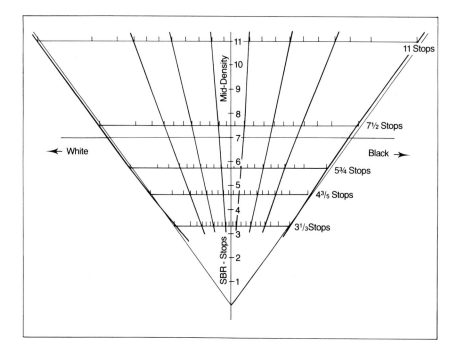

Figure 11-7. If the SBRs are spaced along a central axis according to range and their nominal mid-points are aligned, as shown here, the seven major divisions of the ranges can be connected to form a fan. Each segment of the fan represents a print tone; pure print white is represented by the area outside the fan on the left, pure print black is represented by the area outside the fan on the right. The fan axis—the nominal mid-line—represents average print gray (not the usual 18% "middle gray) which in this case is a reflection density of about 0.9.

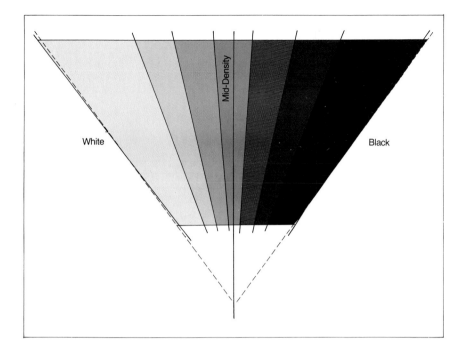

Figure 11-8. Shading the fan stripes shows the tonal gradation more clearly. The seven fan stripe densities increase in increments of about 0.25. Of course the gradation should be continuous from one boundary to the other but this is not practical.

relationship between subject luminance values and print grays but it isn't very accurate or convenient.

The comparison is much more direct and pertinent if the calculator dial of a meter is superimposed over the fan so the luminance numbers and the visible grays can be seen in intimate relationship. We can't use this fan that way, though, because its SBRs are plotted as straight lines and the calculator dial is circular. No problem. Redraw the SBRs on a series of appropriately spaced arcs and reconstruct the fan. Here's how to make a fan to fit your Wonder Wheel sleeve.

Constructing the Fan

First, draw a straight vertical line on a sheet of paper (8½ × 11 is fine) and divide about half its length into 10 or 12 spaces, each 10mm. long. Number these points from bottom to top, starting with the number 4. Next, set your compasses for a radius of 43mm. and draw semicircular arcs through the points marked 4, 7, and 8. The arcs represent SBRs; the numbers indicate the stops in each range. Now, using the luminance scale on the calculator dial as a guide, mark the appropriate number of stops on each of the numbered arcs, centering each range on the vertical line.

Next, draw straight lines through the end points of the 4-stop and 8-stop SBR arcs, extending the lines to intersect on the center axis below the arcs (Fig. 11-9). These boundary lines define the theoretical limits of all the SBRs up to about 10 stops or so. Higher ranges will not quite reach the boundary lines because of the arc curvatures, but don't worry about it now; we'll make a satisfactory compensation for this problem during calibration.

The arcs we just constructed are simply guides. The real SBRs,

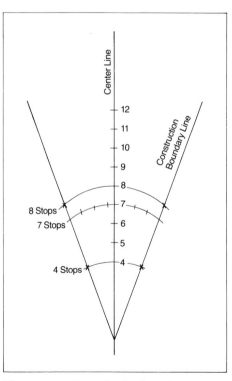

Figure 11-9. To make the fan of grays useful the SBRs must be constructed as curves to match the circumference of the Wonder Wheel calculator dial. Here is the first step in the construction.

139

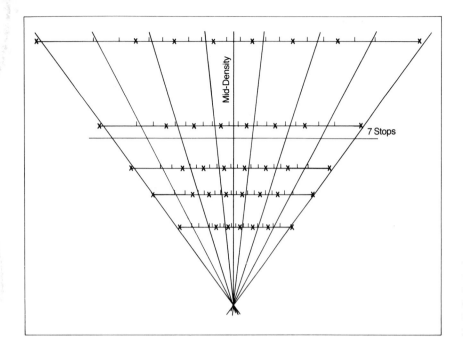

Mid-Density

7 Stops

Figure 11-10. You'll need some guide lines in transferring the stripes from the original fan to the Wonder Wheel fan. Locate the 7-stop SBR on the original fan and use it to divide the fan into 7 1-stop segments.

derived from the film curves, have to be located now. This is easy enough to do; an SBR of 7½ stops, for example, will be drawn on an arc spaced halfway between the 7-stop and 8-stop marks on the central axis.

Now each of the SBR arcs must be divided into its 21 steps, but before you begin, check back through the film and paper curves to be sure you're getting the highlight and shadow ends of the SBRs in the right position: the *top* of the print DR is the shadow end, the *bottom* of the negative DR is the shadow end and the left ends of the SBRs represent shadow values, as they are located under the film curves. The SBRs must be reversed when their steps are transferred to the fan arcs, because we want the *left* margin of the fan to represent highlight tones and the *right* margin to represent shadows.

It will be relatively easy to transfer the SBR divisions to the arcs if some reference lines are provided. I suggest that you construct a 7-stop SBR line in the original fan and, using its divisions as reference points, divide the fan into 7 large stripes (Fig 11-10). Do the same with the arcs, using the divisions of the 7-stop arc as guide points (Fig. 11-11). Now it's fairly easy to transfer the SBR divisions from the straight lines to the arcs, one by one. (Fig. 11-12).

When all the divisions have been transferred, connect the individual points to form the stripes. Mark them with pencil lightly at first, then clean up the lines and eliminate minor irregularities with your french curve and a sharp pencil. The final construction step is shown in Figure 11-13; other fan patterns for various material combinations are given in the Workbook, pages 65-67. Don't be alarmed if the finished fan stripes don't fit neatly and symmetrically into the construction lines. It's normal for the fan to be shifted slightly to the right or left of the center line and the stripes may be slightly curved.

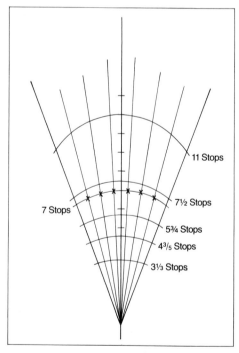

11 Stops

7½ Stops

7 Stops

5¾ Stops

4⅗ Stops

3⅓ Stops

Figure 11-11. Construct the 7-stop arc on the Wonder Wheel fan and use it to divide this fan into 7 1-stop segments. Now the smaller division can be transferred relatively easily from the original fan by simply estimating their relative positions.

The fan now represents the scale of print values which will result from any combination of film exposure and development—within the useful range of the materials—when followed by normal printing (remember, these diagrams have been stylized somewhat and do not accurately represent any real materials). The area outside the fan boundary on the left stands for pure paper white in the print; the space beyond the right hand boundary represents print maximum black, as you have defined it. The fan stripes, when finished, will increase in density from left to right, in this case in uniform increments of about 0.08. The process distortion of tone is indicated by the varying widths of the fan stripes and their slight curvature.

The steps must now be printed. Use the same paper used to make the original print curves for most accurate representation of the print tones, but another paper can be used if its image quality is reasonably similar. There is a distinct advantage to using one paper for all fans because the fan stripe exposures are difficult to compute and they'll be different for different papers. That's a problem you can deal with when you come to it. First you need to make a mask for the fan exposures.

Making the Printing Mask. Trace the fan onto a sheet of thin, opaque paper. The yellow outer envelope that holds Kodak papers is fine. Cut out a piece somewhat larger than the fan dimensions and use carbon paper to make the tracing on the yellow side. Then with a sharp knife or razor blade, cut along each fan stripe border so the individual stripes can be folded back. Don't cut the stripes loose; some of them will be very narrow at the lower end and you'll have to be very careful with the knife. You should be able to extend the cuts down to about the 5-stop arc. There's no point in trying to go further.

Determining the Fan Exposures. You'll have to do some careful testing now to determine the print exposures required to produce the desired uniform increments of print density. The obvious way to do this is to use the step tablet and print it, but that won't work for this purpose. You'll have to provide a very great range of exposures to complete the fan and that means you'll almost certainly have to compensate for reciprocity failure. Also, the final exposure will consist of 21 additive exposure increments and this means there will probably be some errors introduced because of the "intermittency effect." It's best to do this test the hard way—by trial and error.

You'll need a very dim light and a short exposure for the lightest grays so raise your enlarger up, close the lens down to a moderately small aperture, and (with no negative in the carrier) make a geometric test strip on your selected paper, as follows: cover a small section of the paper strip to preserve pure paper white, then expose the remainder of the strip for the selected minimum time, say, 1 second. Cover another small step, to protect the 1-second exposure, and make another exposure *equivalent to the accumulated total exposure of the last step.* Since the last step has had only a 1-second exposure, the second exposure is also 1 second. Covering another small step will protect an accumulated total of 2 seconds, so the next exposure is 2 seconds.

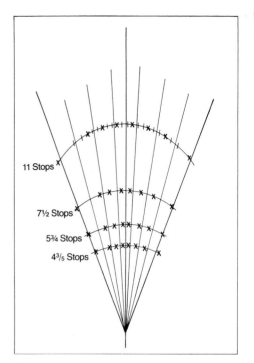

Figure 11-12. Here the construction points are shown. The three lower arcs have been divided into their 7 major stripes. The upper arc has been subdivided into the final 21 steps. When all the arcs have been subdivided, connect the points to form the final 21-step fan.

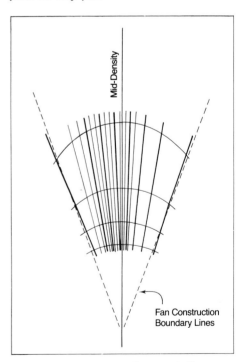

Figure 11-13. Here the partially completed fan is shown. The 7 major segments are shown in heavy lines for clarity.

Again cover a small step, this one bearing exposures of 1 + 1 + 2 = 4 seconds. Give the remainder 4 seconds; next 8, then 16, and so on, always duplicating the accumulated total under the cover sheet. The final sequence will increase uniformly by a factor of 2 and the last step will have received a total equal to twice the last exposure time.

The test strip should cover an exposure range great enough to produce maximum paper black. Develop it fully, fix it well, wash it briefly, and dry it; then read the reflection densities with your spotmeter densitometer. The exposure times and their resulting reflection densities might look like this:

Exposure Time	Reflection Density
1 second	0.0 (paper white)
2	0.0
4	0.0
8	0.12
16	0.42
32	1.0
64	1.53
128	1.75
256	1.82
512	1.87

Plot these values in conventional graph form to display the characteristic curve of the paper under these test conditions (Fig. 11-14). Use

Cut the fan stripes with a sharp knife. This looks difficult but isn't; you'll probably find it easiest to do freehand, as shown here.

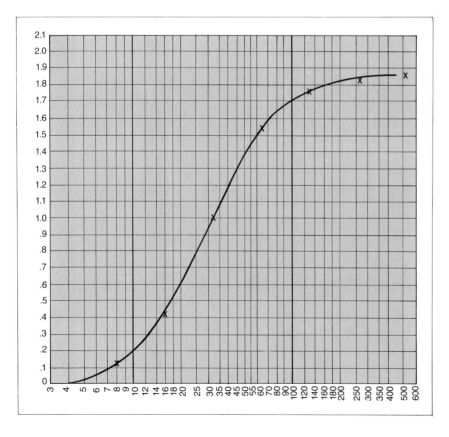

Figure 11-14. The paper curve resulting from a series of short, cumulative exposure times. Sensitized materials don't react normally when exposed this way; contrast is typically reduced substantially and gradation is affected, as shown here.

142

commercially available semi-log paper or use the special form on page 61 of the Workbook. The graph values will be difficult to interpret if plotted on non-log paper.

Dividing the selected paper Dmax value of 1.7 by 2.1 gives us 0.080952 (approximately 0.08), the interval between the steps. It might seem that the density of the first step should be 0.08, but that's not the case. Each of the steps represents an arbitrary division of a continuous gray scale and should, therefore, display the *average* value of its range. The first step, which represents the range from 0.0 to 0.08, should be the average of those values—0.04. The final step, covering the range from about 1.62 to 1.7, should read 1.66 (1.62 + 1.7 = 3.32 ÷ 2 = 1.66). The 21 steps and their desired densities (based on the interval 0.08) are as follows:

Step	Density
1	0.04
2	0.12
3	0.20
4	0.28
5	0.37
6	0.45
7	0.53
8	0.61
9	0.69
10	0.77
11	0.85
12	0.93
13	1.01
14	1.10
15	1.18
16	1.26
17	1.34
18	1.42
19	1.50
20	1.58
21	1.66

Now we can get a rough idea of the necessary exposure times by consulting the graph (Fig. 11-14). Don't be distressed if your graph curve is somewhat different from the "normal" paper curve. The gradation will be affected by the intermittency effect in this test; the curve shape for a single exposure time—as is the usual condition in actual printing—may be different from this one.

Here are the final test exposure times, as estimated from the graph.

Step	Density	Individual Exposures	Time
1	0.04	5½ seconds	5½ seconds
2	0.12	2¾	8¼
3	0.20	2	10¼
4	0.28	2¼	12½
5	0.37	2½	15
6	0.45	2	17
7	0.53	2	19
8	0.61	1½	20½
9	0.69	2	22½
10	0.77	2	24½
11	0.85	2½	27
12	0.93	3	30
13	1.01	2½	32½
14	1.10	3½	36
15	1.18	3	39
16	1.26	4	43
17	1.34	5	48
18	1.42	6	54
19	1.50	7	61
20	1.58	10	71
21	1.66	17	88

The exposure data should be tested before applying it to the fan itself, and because the lighter values are the most critical, it's wise to make a preliminary test of the first few steps. Using the same enlarger settings, prepare a test strip and after covering a small section of it to retain pure paper white, expose the rest of the strip for 5½ seconds. Cover a bit more of the strip and give the remainder 2¾ seconds, then continue the sequence with exposures of 2, 2¼, 2½ 2, 2, 1½, and 2.

Process the strip normally, wash briefly, and dry. Then read the densities of the 9 steps. If they are not very close to the target densities, adjust the exposures as seems appropriate and make another test. Don't expect perfection here; be satisfied that coming close to the ideal values of most of the steps is a sort of technical triumph, and represents greater precision than you'll be able to maintain in actual field conditions.

Printing the Fan. When the exposure testing is done, the actual fan exposures are comparatively easy. Fold back the right-hand border area of the fan mask as shown so that area will receive saturation exposure for absolute Dmax. Leave the left-hand border area in contact with the paper throughout the sequence of exposures to preserve maximum paper white. Now tape the mask down to the printing paper—outside the image area—to avoid slippage, and fold the fan mask strips back carefully to avoid tearing any of them. It's convenient to use a few small weights to keep the mask in close contact with the paper. If you're working on a metal easel you can use small bar magnets for the same purpose.

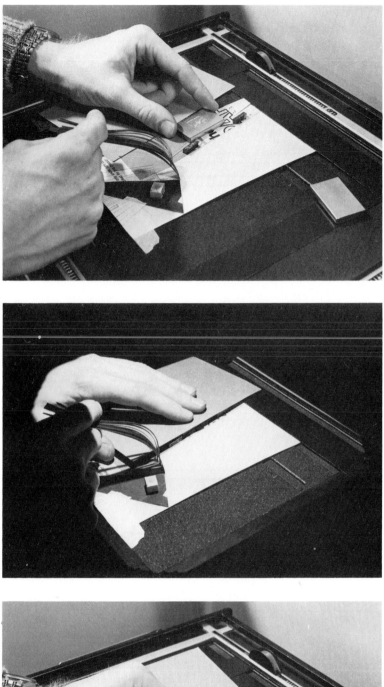

The fan is exposed progressively from left to right. The wide right-hand margin strip is folded down permanently so the fan border area will reach maximum black.

During the actual exposure the previously exposed stripes should be protected with an opaque cover to avoid possible light leakage between the mask strips. It's a good idea to move the easel a little between exposures so that dust and lint on the enlarger condenser surfaces won't produce noticeable patterns on the fan stripes.

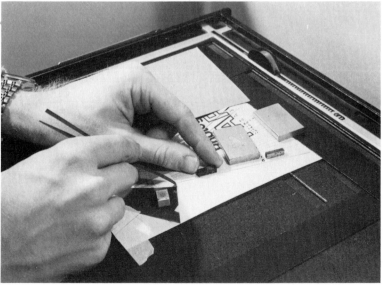

After each exposure a mask strip is folded down and held in place with small weights or magnets. The larger weights keep the fan flat and provide support for the cardboard cover during the exposures.

Make the first exposure with only the left border area covered, then fold down the first strip and make the second exposure. Be sure the strip fits snugly against the edge of the border mask to avoid light leakage. Continue this procedure, one strip at a time, until the whole fan has been exposed; then fog the right-hand border area thoroughly to produce full paper black. Process the print and dry it. If there are signs of double imaging or blurring of the stripes, you are probably either allowing the mask strips to move during exposure or not keeping them completely flat. Their alignment is critical, and it will probably take a few trials to get it perfect. Keep track of the densities, too. If the first trial isn't as good as it should be, make the appropriate adjustments and redo it. The fan will not be very useful if the densities are not quite close to the ideal values, or if the stripes are uneven, blurred, or outlined with light or dark edges.

If this has sounded like a horrendous procedure, it's because it is. On the other hand, if done well, the fan will be extremely useful. If you need encouragement to go on, consider the fact that you can use the same exposure series for all other fans you make on this same paper—ones for other films, for example. Different contrast grades or different types of papers will require new tests.

Preparing the Fan Slide. To complete the fan for use, dry mount it on thin cardboard and cut it to fit the sleeve. This is an important step; if it isn't cut straight, it will introduce exposure errors into your data. Do it this way: first, determine the width required to fit your Wonder Wheel sleeve. If an existing slide fits well, measure its width. If not, or if you don't have a slide, cut a piece of the slide cardboard material to the desired width by trial and error, and measure it. Mark this width on the new fan slide, being sure to keep the center axis line centered. Cut the slide very slightly wider than the marked dimensions so that the edges can be sanded down for snug fit and smooth operation. Wax the edges lightly with paraffin, and polish them with a cloth or tissue. The slide should move easily, without appreciable lateral play. Push it down into the sleeve until the outer fan boundaries span 14 or 15 stops on the calculator dial, then mark the slide ends for trimming. When finished, the slide should fit neatly into the sleeve.

Fan Calibration: Finding the SBRs. The fan can now be calibrated for exposure correction and development information. If you marked the center line of the slide during construction, check it now to see that it is accurate. To do this easily, set some mark on the calculator dial on the center line and watch the line as you withdraw the slide slowly. If the line remains aligned with the mark as the slide is moved in or out, it is usable for calibration and reference. If not, it will cause some slight error in exposure. Remake the slide if the line moves off-center by more than $1/3$ stop as the slide is withdrawn.

Now calibrate for the SBRs. Pull the slide out until the outside boundary lines of the fan span exactly 5 stops on the calculator dial. Holding the slide firmly to prevent it from slipping, turn the Wonder Wheel over, make a mark opposite the pointer in the SBR window, and label it 5. Push the slide in until the fan boundary lines indicate a range

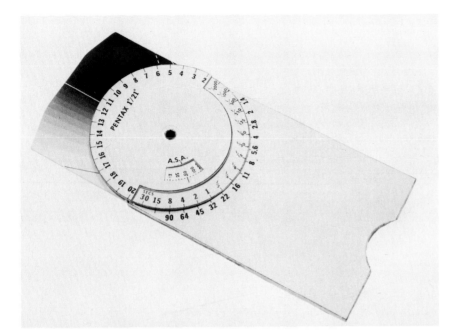

The Wonder Wheel, assembled.

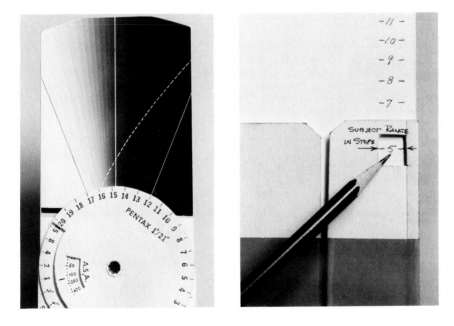

Left: Position the slide so the fan boundary lines span exactly 5 stops. Right: Without moving the slide, turn the sleeve over and mark 5 in the Subject Range window, as shown.

of 6 stops. Similarly mark and label 6 in the SBR window. Do this for SBRs up to or through about 14 stops. You can also mark ⅓ or ½ stops if you want to.

You'll notice, if you remove the slide and inspect the SBR numbers, that they're spaced quite evenly up to about the 10-stop level. Then the spacing gradually decreases. This is the compensation for the arc curvature, mentioned previously. It's normal and necessary for high-range accuracy.

Exposure compensation is necessary, too, just as it is in the Incident and Zone Systems. Let's take a few minutes for one last review of this important subject.

Exposure Compensation: Review

In all three systems the exposure adjustments for changes in SBR are designed to maintain a uniform minimum negative density level for all conditions of development. In the Incident System, this is accomplished by basing the exposure settings on incident light measurements of the subject shadows and applying a further correction based on the relative positions of the characteristic curve speed points, measured at a little below mid-density level. Metering the shadow illumination, instead of using an overall average reading, guarantees an exposure sufficient to record subject shadow detail, regardless of the SBR; the additional exposure adjustment—made by changing the effective film speed setting—is sufficient to counteract any speed point shift that may be caused by the required development, and maintain the Dmin at the desired level.

In the Zone System, the exposure is also based on the lower zone luminance by zone placement—setting the meter pointer on a value higher than the desired one by some fixed number of stops. In the description given previously (see Chapter 8), the recommended Zone III placement was achieved by setting the normal pointer (Zone V) 2 stops above the subject luminance value on the meter calculator dial. This move underexposes the metered subject luminance by 2 stops without regard for the development conditions and leaves the fate of Dmin in doubt for subjects of other than normal SBR.

If the subject range is normal (7 stops) the 2-stop separation between the normal pointer and the Zone III setting is normal and the desired Dmin value—corresponding to the lower boundary of Zone II—will fall where it belongs, 1½ stops below Zone III. For longer or shorter SBRs, however, the 2-stop separation is not in correct proportion to the total range and compensation is again a two-stage procedure. First, the 2-*stop* space between Zone III and the normal pointer must be stretched or shrunk to become two *zones* ($2/7$ of the total SBR) and second, exposure compensation, based on the film curve speed points, must be made for each condition of development. In practice, as previously pointed out, these two compensation steps can be done as one if the ASA speed correction is made on the curves at the selected low zone level (Zone III in the examples given) rather than at the usual Dmin level of 0.1 over B + F.

Wonder Wheel exposure compensation for changing SBRs follows a similar pattern. First, the determination of subject range is done by individual placement of luminance readings opposite selected fan stripe grays, without regard for meter calibration or camera exposure. The Wonder Wheel calculator automatically averages all these luminance placements and, at this first stage, simply displays the relationships of luminances and print grays within the total selected SBR.

Exposure correction can again be thought of as including two steps: the 3½ stops (approximately) between minimum and middle luminance values (which is built into the meter calibration) must be stretched or shrunk to accommodate the SBR if it is other than the normal 7 stops. Then, additional correction must be made to take care of the effective film speed change resulting from nonstandard development. In practice these adjustments can also be made as one step, but in this case—because the fan is approximately symmetrical and, therefore, tends to hold print middle gray at a nearly constant value regardless of SBR—the effective film speeds are found from speed points on the characteristic curves at the *print mid-density* level.

One further step is necessary. The design of the slides requires that exposure correction be accomplished by rotating the calculator dial rather than adjusting the film speed setting in the ASA window as has been recommended for the Incident and Zone Systems (the Wonder Wheel uses the manufacturer's assigned film speeds). This is done, as has been previously described, by turning the dial to move the luminance value, which appears over the broken line on the fan, into alignment with the central solid line. This adjustment, coupled with appropriate development, corrects the effective film exposure for Dmin, regardless of SBR.

Untitled photograph by David Bartlett. Exposure and development determined with the Wonder Wheel and a Luna-Pro meter. Data not available. Courtesy of the photographer.

149

Fan Calibration: Effective Film Speeds

Now back to the calibration. To locate the broken exposure correction line on the fan, first consult the film curves and compile a simple chart plotting SBRs against effective film speed at the print mid-density level of each curve (Fig. 11-15a). The actual values of effective film speed are not important; we need only the extent of their deviation from normal, expressed in stops (Fig. 11-15b). This exposure correction can now be transferred to the fan slide. Consider the fan center line to stand for the normal ASA speed. Now position the slide to indicate the lowest range—4³/₅ stops. The chart shows the speed for this range to be about +⅝ or ⅝ stop greater than normal. Using the calculator dial markings as a guide for the stop intervals, move to the left of the center line about ⅝ stop and mark the fan lightly near the edge of the dial (Fig. 11-16). Now set the slide at 5⅓ stop range—considered normal on the chart—and place a mark on the center line at the edge of the dial. Now move the slide to the 7½ stop range, and indicate the correction shift (−1⅔ stops) placing the mark this time on the right side of the center line to indicate a speed decrease.

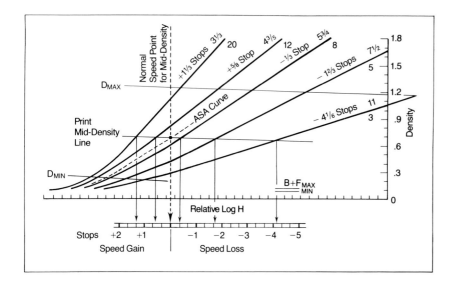

Do the same for one or more of the higher ranges, then remove the slide and connect the points with a broken line, using your french curve to keep the line smooth and even. If you have difficulty making a legible mark with black ink, use white ink or scratch the line through the print emulsion with a sharp instrument. It's helpful to emphasize the right-hand boundary line the same way.

The slide is now complete and ready for use. Be sure to label it with the names of the materials it represents and, if you want to add developing information to the slide itself, you can draw an SBR-vs.-developing-time chart on the back of the slide.

If you are a confirmed Zone System addict and feel lost without some reference to N-numbers, you can include them on the slide, too. It's a fairly simple matter to relate N-numbers to the SBRs in stops, by referring to the characteristic curves and going through the construc-

Figure 11-15a. Both the Incident System and Zone System require that effective film speed (EFS) values for other-than-normal subject ranges be determined by using the normal (7-stop) curve as reference. This is because both systems are dependent on the meter calculator dial and the meter dial is inflexibly calibrated for the normal 7-stop range only. Because the Wonder Wheel replaces the meter as a calculating device, and depends on it only for light-measuring, the Wheel can be related directly to the ASA standard. The ASA speed number is set into the Wheel calculator and the ASA curve is used as the reference for determining EFS values for all subject ranges. The Wonder Wheel design dictates that speed correction be based on the print mid-range density level. Actual speed numbers are not important here; simply calculate the speed gain or loss in stops.

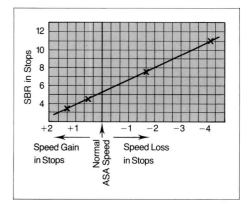

Figure 11-15b. Plot the speed variation against SBR, as shown.

tion steps described in Chapter 8. Remember, though, the N-numbers refer to specific pairs of zones and bear no fixed relationship to the Wonder Wheel fan or the exposure or developing information it contains. I would advise you not to mix the two systems. If you're comfortable with the Zone System, use it; if you like the Wonder Wheel features, use the wheel. Either approach will work well but they work differently; attempts to blend the two may get you into trouble.

Review Chapter 10 for operating instructions. If you don't get consistent results with the wheel, remember it's only a calculating device; it supplies the data, you supply the brains. If you have tested the materials correctly, used the wheel intelligently, and made the right decisions, you'll get good results.

There are two hazards we haven't discussed: *reciprocity failure* and *flare*. Neither is really predictable or controllable but, since you'll almost certainly have to contend with them sooner or later, you should know what to expect. Chapter 12 discusses some ways to identify and compensate for flare and reciprocity problems; then, for fine tuning your procedures and wringing the last little bit of quality out of your prints, I'll suggest some adjustments, corrections, and refinements that you may find useful.

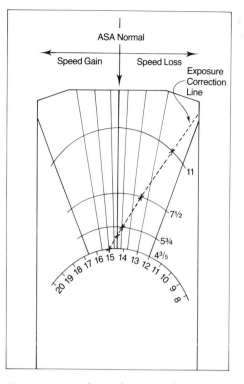

Figure 11-16. This is how speed compensation is incorporated into the fan slides. Marks on the left of the fan center line indicate a speed gain; marks on the right indicate speed loss. The measurements to right and left are made in stops, using the calculator dial as reference.

CHAPTER

12

Fine Tuning

As I've mentioned several times, it's impossible to exert absolute control over the photographic process. Don't expect every negative to be perfect and don't be dismayed if some of your prints lack the magic you planned for them. Errors are possible at every stage and occasionally they'll combine with disastrous results. In general, though, if each process step is controlled within reasonable limits you can assume that technical failures will be infrequent. The testing procedures presented in preceding chapters should give you this kind of control, at least for subjects of normal or near-normal range.

Extra compensation may be necessary for unusual subject conditions. *Reciprocity failure* may affect films exposed for very long or very short times and *flare* will undoubtedly affect pictures made against the light, pictures taken with an uncoated or dirty lens, and pictures of subjects of extreme contrast.

"Failure" of the Reciprocity Law

The reciprocity law states that exposure effect varies uniformly with changes in either time or light intensity or—if you prefer—exposure effect will remain constant if the product of exposure time and light intensity is constant. This relationship is valid and predictable in most situations but when light intensity on the film surface is reduced below the "normal" minimum or increased beyond the "normal" maximum, the emulsion effectively loses sensitivity and the exposure effect is not as great as it should be. The emulsion, in other words, has a preferred range of light intensities, within which it behaves predictably. For light intensities outside this range it loses speed and the reciprocity law "fails."

Film illumination can't be measured directly but it does influence exposure time. Consequently, it's customary to relate reciprocity failure to time because when exposures must be either very short or very long we *recognize* the need to compensate. But illumination, not time, is the important factor, as demonstrated by the fact that high illumination levels cause a reduction in image contrast whereas very low levels of film illumination cause an increase in image contrast.

If this doesn't make sense at first, think about it for a minute: film loses sensitivity in extremely bright light; the image highlights are brighter than the shadows; therefore, the highlights are proportionately less well-formed than the shadows and contrast is reduced. At very low illumination levels sensitivity also diminishes; the shadows are less well-illuminated than the highlights; therefore, the shadows are proportionately less well-formed than the highlights and contrast is increased.

The image shadows and highlights receive identical exposure *times* under all conditions; only intensity varies. Therefore, reciprocity failure must be due primarily to variations in illumination rather than in time.

Since reciprocity failure affects both image density and contrast, its compensation must include adjustment of both exposure and development. Unfortunately, "failure" isn't an entirely predictable effect. Not all films react the same way to exposure extremes, and other factors are at work too. Substantial temperature variations are known to influence reciprocity failure, and it's also probable that film age has some effect. For these reasons, compensation charts and tables are usually vague. Kodak's recommendation for most of their films goes like this:

If exposure time is:	Open aperture	OR	Use this exposure time	AND	Adjust development by
$1/1000$ second	—		$1/1000$ second		+10%
$1/100$	—		$1/100$		—
$1/10$	—		$1/10$		—
1	1 stop		2 seconds		−10%
10	2 stops		50 seconds		−20%
100	3 stops		1200 seconds		−30%

In my experience these recommendations are a little excessive but they are easy to remember.

Testing for Reciprocity Effects

It would seem logical to test for reciprocity effects by contact printing the step tablet on film under the enlarger, as was done in making the original film tests. This, however, is not a good idea for two reasons: first, the warm-up time of the enlarger bulb (especially low-voltage, high-current types) will not permit accurate timing of the shortest exposure required ($1/10$ second) and, second, stray light from the enlarger will almost certainly have an appreciable effect on the exposure at the longest times, and the test accuracy will be questionable. It's best to do this test series in the camera, simply photographing the transilluminated step tablet.

You can tape the step tablet directly onto a fluorescent tube for this test. First take a reading of the light source itself to be sure it will permit an exposure of at least $1/500$ second at the maximum aperture of your lens. Then tape the step tablet to the glass and mask it on all sides with black paper to reduce flare effects. The basic exposure for the step tablet should normally be about 5 stops greater than the raw light reading, but there are two things to consider before starting the test series. First, the initial exposure time should be $1/10$ second for easy calculation of the results; second, if you move in close enough to get a usefully large image of the step tablet, you'll probably have to increase the indicated exposure to compensate for *bellows extension*. If you're not familiar with this problem and its solution, see the appendix, pages 173-174.

The individual steps of the step tablet should be at least ⅛ inch wide on the negative. Calculate the bellows extension factor, then consult your meter. Let's assume your meter reading of the raw light source suggests a camera setting of $1/10$ second at f/64. You must overexpose at least 5 stops—6 is better—to provide a good step tablet image and the bellows factor will add, say, another 1½ stops. That's a total exposure increase of 6½ or 7½ stops. A 6½ stop increase indicates an exposure of $1/10$ second between f/5.6 and f/8. That's usable, but f/5.6 is probably safer. If your shutter provides a $1/10$ speed, your basic exposure will be $1/10$ at f/5.6. If you don't have $1/10$, use the ⅛ second setting.

This reciprocity test is based on the assumption that exposure times of $1/10$ second, 1 second, 10 seconds, and 100 seconds will all provide the same film image density if the film illumination is decreased proportionately. The film illumination could be controlled with the lens diaphragm if it were calibrated accurately enough, and if it provided enough range, neither of which is conceivable. A better method is to reduce the illumination with *neutral density filters*. These are much more accurate and they are available in a variety of strengths to cover a wide range.

The actual test is simple. Make one exposure at $1/10$ second at f/5.6; one at 1 second at f/5.6 with a ND 1.0 filter over the camera lens; one at 10 seconds with a ND 2.0 filter; and one at 100 seconds with a ND 3.0 filter. If you don't have a $1/10$ second speed on your shutter, follow this procedure: first exposure, ⅛ second at f/5.6; second, 1 second at f/5.6 with a ND 0.9 filter; third, 10 seconds with ND 0.9 + 1.0 filters; fourth, 100 seconds with ND 0.9 + 2.0 filters. Although it's possible to make up the desired neutral densities by superimposing several filters as required, some light loss is occasioned by the added surfaces of the gelatin sheets. It's best, if possible, to use single filters for each density, but the error won't be great if only two are combined.

Process all the test films together normally, then read the negative densities and plot them against the original step tablet densities in the usual manner. The resulting curves will probably look something like Figure 12-1. It's safe to assume the $1/10$-second curve is not affected significantly by reciprocity failure. By comparison, then, the 1-second curve indicates a speed loss of about ⅔ stop, with no appreciable contrast increase. The 10-second curve shows a speed loss of about

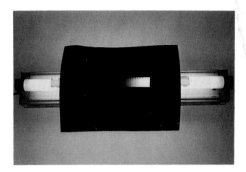

It's safe and convenient to do reciprocity testing in the camera. Mask your step tablet with black paper and tape it onto a fluorescent tube to provide a bright target, as shown here. Be sure the mask is large enough to cover the entire image field, and use a deep lens shade to reduce flare.

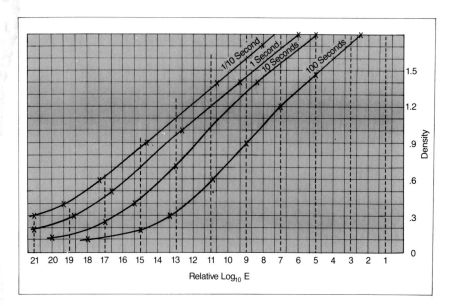

Figure 12-1. *Typical reciprocity effect curves for a medium-speed film exposed for times of ¹/₁₀ second, 1 second, 10 seconds, and 100 seconds.*

1⁵/₆ stops and a slight increase in gradient and the 100-second curve is affected even more seriously.

It's also interesting to see the effect on the curve shape. Reciprocity failure, on this film at least, extends the curve toe dramatically. This has some important implications: since conditions which might require a 100-second exposure are frequently contrasty, it's quite likely the reduced shadow contrast due to reciprocity failure will be further reduced by the shortened developing time (recommended to keep overall image contrast under control) causing a serious loss of shadow detail. Even if the exposure is adequately compensated, the lengthening of the curve toe and the increased mid-range gradient suggest a distinct alteration in gradation toward murky shadows and accented mid-tone contrast.

The determination of developing times for reciprocity failure compensation involves some guesswork. It would, of course, be possible to run sets of characteristic curves at each of the test exposure times but that seems unnecessarily scientific. It's accurate enough, in practice, to estimate the correction like this: first, determine the average gradient of each of the curves. In a hypothetical example:

for ¹/₁₀ second negative the $\bar{G}$ is	0.6
1 second	0.6
10 seconds	0.68
100 seconds	0.76

Then divide the actual values of $\bar{G}$ by the expected value (we'll assume 0.6 was the target value) to find the percentage of increase due to reciprocity failure:

for ¹/₁₀ second neg.	0.6 ÷ 0.6 = 1
1 second	0.6 ÷ 0.6 = 1
10 seconds	0.68 ÷ 0.6 = 1.13
100 seconds	0.76 ÷ 0.6 = 1.27

156

Now, because reciprocity failure causes an increase in negative $\bar{G}$, we'll have to develop for some lower than desired value to actually achieve the desired one. How much lower? Divide the desired $\bar{G}$ value—in this case 0.6—by the appropriate percentage (in decimal form) to find out. If you've exposed a sheet of film for 100 seconds and if you want to reach an actual $\bar{G}$ of 0.6, divide 0.6 by 1.27:

$$0.6 \div 1.27 = 0.47$$

From a $\bar{G}$-vs.-developing-time chart, pick the time listed for 0.47 and develop the film (Fig. 12-2). The negative's $\bar{G}$ should measure approximately 0.6. Two cautions: don't apply this correction to the developing *time* itself—work with the $\bar{G}$ values; then consult the chart to find the developing time. Also, this *procedure* is valid for all films but the *numbers* used in this example are not. Test each film you're interested in.

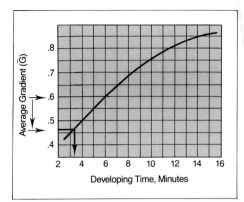

Figure 12-2. *In this hypothetical case the original developing time (6 minutes) for an average gradient of 0.6 must be reduced to 3:20 for an indicated $\bar{G}$ of 0.47. Reciprocity effects will restore the negative DR if exposure is calculated correctly.*

Testing for Flare

Flare effect is even more uncertain than is reciprocity failure but should be considered and compensated for as well as is possible. This test is not precise, but it will give you some idea of the seriousness of the problem.

Find a large cardboard box—at least 12 inches along its smallest dimension, and cut a 3 inch or 4 inch hole in one side. Paint the inside of the box, and the area around the hole on the outside, matte black. Tape the box shut and seal the cracks and corners with black tape, if necessary, to keep light from entering. Then contrive a deep "sunshade" to protect the opening from direct light and paint it black, too (Fig. 12-3). You have just created a photographic "black hole."

Although some light will enter the box and a tiny fraction of it will be reflected back through the opening, the amount is negligible. For test purposes you can consider the opening to be totally dark. If the box is placed in the subject area and photographed with normal exposure, the negative image of the box opening should, therefore, be clear except for B + F density. Any density greater than film B + F must be due to some influence other than image light. The most likely cause is flare.

To estimate the amount of flare your camera and lens generate, place the box in the shadow area of a normal-contrast subject and expose normally. Similarly, test a low-contrast subject condition and at least one high-contrast situation. The most serious flare will probably occur when a large brilliant area of the subject is very close to, or actually surrounds, the test area. This sort of condition exists when you attempt to retain detail in a silhouette portrait, or a photograph of a dark-toned room interior, including the windows, by natural light alone.

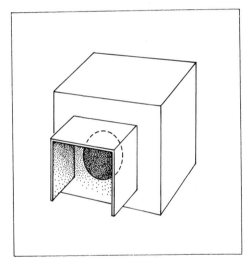

Figure 12-3. *The flare test box—a photographic black hole.*

Compensating Your Film Curves for Flare

Measure the test subject ranges carefully, and when you've developed the negatives, read the "black hole" densities of each and record them like this:

Subject Range	Black Hole Density	B + F	Flare Density
5 stops	0.1	0.1	0.0
7 stops	0.13	0.11	0.02
9 stops	0.15	0.12	0.03
12 stops	0.23	0.14	0.09

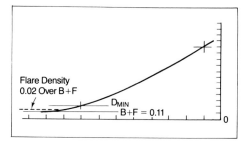

Figure 12-4a. *Here is a normal range (7 stops) film curve with flare density indicated as a dotted line at 0.02 over B + F.*

Then consult the film curves. In Figure 12-4a the 7-stop curve has been drawn alone for purposes of illustration and the B + F density (0.11) has been indicated. The flare density (0.02) is also indicated as a dotted line. If we are going to include the flare exposure effect in the characteristic curve, we must know the amount of exposure the flare produced. There is no way to measure the flare intensity inside the camera, but since it has resulted in a density increase (in this example) of 0.02 over B + F, it must have been identical with the amount of *image* light that resulted in a similar density. Extend the flare density line to the right along the exposure axis until it intersects the curve. At that point the effective flare exposure can be found on the exposure axis (Fig. 12-4b).

Let's say the image exposure at this point equals x. Then the flare exposure is also x, and the total exposure is 2x. This is the first step, but the flare must be added to all the image densities, assuming it was uniformly distributed over the entire image area. Moving along the exposure axis one step at a time we can label the image exposures alone as x, 2x, 4x, 8x, 16x, etc. The flare exposure, however, is a constant x at all points. The totals, therefore, corresponding to each image density step are:

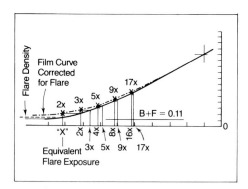

Figure 12-4b. *Flare exposure must be equivalent to the image exposure (x) which results in a similar density, in this case 0.02. At the point on the film curve where image density is 0.02, therefore, image exposure (x) plus the identical flare exposure (x) produces an exposure total of 2x.*

Image Exposure Alone	Flare Exposure	Image + Flare Exposure Total
x	x	2x
2x	x	3x
4x	x	5x
8x	x	9x
16x	x	17x

The resulting densities are found by plotting a new characteristic curve, using the image + flare exposure totals instead of the normal image exposure values; for example, the image normal density for an exposure of 8x is replaced by the density for 9x and the normal 16x density is replaced by the density resulting from 17x exposure (Fig. 12-4c).

Each of the curves in the family can be adjusted to display the effect of flare, as described above, but this modified curve family should be viewed with some suspicion. Flare is not necessarily consistent. You

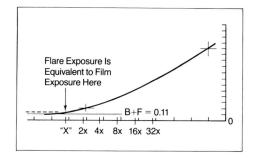

Figure 12-4c. *Flare exposure is constant but image exposure increases to the right along the exposure axis, doubling at every interval of 0.3. At image exposure intervals of x, 2x, 4x, 8x, and 16x, then, the total image-plus-flare exposure is 2x, 3x, 5x, 9x, and 17x. If the image densities for these values of exposure are substituted for the densities of the unflared exposures, a new series of image density points is found. Connecting these points produces a film curve which displays the combined effect of image and flare light.*

Untitled photograph by David Bartlett. Exposure and development determined by use of a Luna-Pro meter and the Wonder Wheel. Data unavailable. Courtesy of the photographer.

can be sure of two things though: all cameras produce some flare, and flare effect will increase if subject contrast (SBR) increases.

Flare increases shadow density dramatically but much of the increase is useless because shadow *contrast* is seriously reduced. If you want to recalibrate, select the Dmin level on each curve "by eye," marking the curve at what you consider to be the lower limit of useful gradient. In this way you'll probably find there is some slight increase in SBR at each developing time and there may be some usable film speed increase but it will not be great unless you're willing to give up some shadow separation.

My recommendation: take every practical measure to exclude flare from the camera when you expose the film, then live with the resulting negative. Adjusting film exposure and development in an attempt to compensate for flare probably won't help much and may actually make things worse. Overexposure, in particular, should be avoided if flare conditions are obviously serious.

Although modern lenses are thoroughly coated to reduce flare and camera manufacturers go to great lengths to subdue internal reflections in both lenses and camera bodies, flare has not always been considered undesirable. Photographers of a couple of generations ago relied on flare effects to reduce the contrast of very long-range subjects and considered the added shadow density a virtue in spite of the related veiling of shadow details. Today we occasionally induce flare deliberately, when subject contrast seems to be unworkably high, by using some sort of diffusing filter over the camera lens or by "flashing" the film, that is, by exposing the film to dim light briefly, before (or sometimes after) the image exposure.

Ideally, the flashing exposure should be great enough to bring the sensitive silver salts almost to the threshold of latent image formation. The emulsion can then respond usefully to lower levels of image light than would normally be required and shadow density, after development, is greater than usual. Since the effect is most apparent in the shadow areas, film speed is effectively increased to some extent and image contrast is reduced. This technique is rediscovered periodically and featured in the popular magazines as another way of "hypersensitizing" film. It does in fact work in some cases but it's difficult to control the pre-exposure accurately. Too little pre-exposure doesn't have much effect and too much will cause a general fog level which, like camera flare, may affect image quality adversely.

In practice, film can be flashed effectively for contrast reduction by exposing it to a gray card, purposely unfocused. The exposure should be sufficient to place the gray in about Zone 0 or Zone I at the most. The same film is then exposed to the subject light for a little less than the normal time, and the combined exposures produce the desired latent image. Depending on the type of film and the accuracy of the pre-exposure, the gain in effective film speed can be appreciable and contrast reduction, in the form of increased shadow density, is frequently substantial. This technique is sometimes useful in taming the inherent high contrast of some Polaroid films (such as Type 52); in this application pre-flashing can sometimes reveal shadow details that are

Top left: Polaroid Type 52 film rendered this contrasty subject dramatically, with some loss of deep shadow detail. Top right: With image exposure reduced ⅓ stop and a pre-exposure sufficient to place a gray card image in Zone 0 (5 stops underexposed), the shadows are lightened enough to reveal detail and texture without affecting the highlights appreciably. Overall contrast is obviously reduced. Left: When the pre-exposure is increased 1 stop (placing the gray card value in Zone 1) the print is unpleasantly gray and the shadows, although well detailed, are veiled and hazy.

almost invisible in a normally exposed and normally processed Polaroid print.

The benefits are not as great with ordinary films. Some speed gain is possible, under ideal conditions, and shadow densities are increased, but shadow contrast suffers. In general, pre-flashing is said to be more effective than flashing after the image exposure but in my experience the difference is negligible. Whether either of these techniques is valuable for you, only you can tell; try them and see.

Film Development Variations

Flare and controlled flashing both extend the toe of the film characteristic curve and, therefore, alter image gradation. The curve can also be altered by process manipulation, such as *divided development*. The familiar *water-bath* technique is a useful example. The film is placed in the developer and agitated until development commences, then drained briefly and allowed to soak quietly in a tray of plain water until the developer contained in the emulsion is exhausted. The sequence is then repeated until the desired density range has been attained.

Water-Bath Development

Water-bath development tends to restrain highlight contrast while retaining shadow detail, as shown graphically in Figure 12-5. This technique works best with sheet film and is less effective with roll film, especially the fine-grain, thin emulsion types. This sort of contrast-limiting development is sometimes called *compensating* development and a similar effect can be obtained by using very highly diluted *one-shot* developers, such as Rodinal™ or Kodak's HC-110™ with minimal agitation.

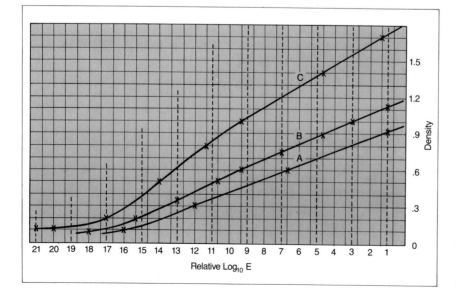

Figure 12-5. Water-bath development reduces negative contrast, retarding developer action in the middle-tone and highlight areas of the image. These curves illustrate the effect of water-bath development on Plus-X sheet film, in D-76, diluted 1:1. The films were pre-soaked in plain water for 1 minute, then agitated continuously in the diluted developer for 30 seconds, and transferred to a tray of plain water where they were allowed to stand without agitation for 1 minute. This developer/water-bath sequence was repeated as follows: Curve A: 7 cycles (total time in developer, 3½ minutes; total time in water bath, 7 minutes). Curve B: 10 cycles. Curve C: 18 cycles.

Compensating development is generally thought to be more effective than it actually is, but it does have some uses. You should probably be familiar with the techniques in case you run into a subject of such formidable contrast that ordinary controls are inadequate.

Divided Development

If the reducing agent and accelerator of a normal developer are mixed as separate solutions and used in sequence, they can provide a significant compensating action. Most such formulas suggest Metol, usually preserved with a little sulfite, as the first bath, followed by a mild solution of borax or sodium metaborate. Kodak's D-23 formula, a useful developer in its own right, makes a good first bath:

Elon (Metol)	7.5 gms.
Sodium sulfite	100.0 gms.
Water	1.0 liter

Agitate films constantly in this solution for 2 minutes, then, without rinsing or draining, immerse them in:

Kodalk (or sodium metaborate)	10.0 gms.
Water	1.0 liter

Do not agitate in the second bath. Development will be complete after about 3 minutes. Divided development of this sort is not much affected by temperature variations, within reasonable limits. Image contrast and density can be affected slightly by varying development times but, by their nature, developers of this kind resist controls. Any significant changes in the characteristics of the developer will require changes in the chemical strengths and proportions.

Two-bath development typically produces a hump in the film curve at about the Zone V level, as shown in Figure 12-6. When

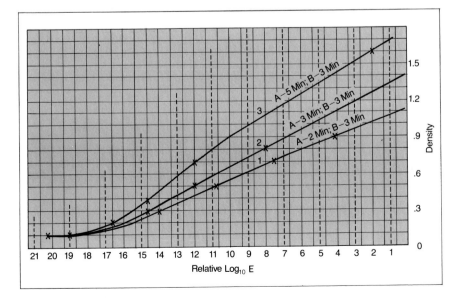

Figure 12-6. Typical two-bath (divided development) curves. Film (1) was agitated constantly in solution A (developer) for 2 minutes, then transferred without draining to solution B (accelerator) and allowed to stand without agitation for 3 minutes. Curve (2): solution A, 3 minutes; solution B, 3 minutes. Curve (3): solution A, 5 minutes; solution B, 3 minutes.

163

significant, this can result in a noticeable increase in shadow density and contrast and a reduction in mid-tone contrast. The very high values are affected, too, since compensation tends to emphasize the shoulder characteristic of the curve. This may or may not be apparent in the image, depending on the subject range and the position of the useful image highlights on the film curve.

Altering Paper Contrast: Pre-exposure

Image gradation can be manipulated to some extent in printing, too. Different pairings of film and paper types can produce different effects; print development can be modified to alter image color, density and contrast; and the image can be doctored by various post-development treatments. Although it's easy to control print contrast by changing paper grades (or filters, in the case of variable-contrast papers), there are times when an intermediate grade of contrast is appropriate. Variable-contrast papers will respond to mixed filtration—part of the exposure through one filter, part through another—but graded papers can't be controlled this way. There are at least two ways to manage them, though. Pre-exposure will reduce contrast and increase speed of papers, just as it does with film. Paper contrast can also be altered by changes in developer composition.

You'll have to devise your own technique for pre-exposure but it's a fairly simple procedure. Provide a dim white light in your darkroom—a "bullet" safelight with the safelight filter removed can be bounced off the ceiling or a large white or gray card to illuminate the workspace. Turn off the room light and lay a strip of printing paper, emulsion up, on the table surface. Cover a section of it with an opaque card and turn on the fogging light for, say, 1 second. Then cover a bit more of the strip and expose for another second. Repeat this procedure until you have exposed 6 or 8 sections of the strip, then turn out the fogging light and develop the strip in safelight.

If all the steps except the unexposed one are obviously grayed, the light was too bright. Substitute a smaller bulb or restrict the light in some way, and repeat the test. If none of the steps show any sign of tone, the light is not bright enough; use a larger bulb or bounce the light from a more reflective surface, or move the light closer to the workspace. If the paper shows a visible tone for exposure times of, say, 10, 9, 8, and 7 seconds, but none for the shorter exposure times, the test is useful. Pre-expose a full sheet of paper for 5 or 6 seconds, in this example, and compare it with an unflashed sheet in actual printing.

This test strip, exposed to a dim white light for times of 2, 4, 8, 16, and 32 seconds, and developed normally, shows a barely perceptible trace of tone for the 8-second exposure. Eight seconds, therefore, is too much pre-exposure for contrast control; the maximum useful pre-exposure for this test condition turned out to be 4 seconds. More than that produced visibly fogged highlights.

You will probably find that the contrast of the pre-flashed sheet is substantially reduced but the print may show signs of degraded highlights. The maximum useful pre-exposure can reduce print contrast by at least a half paper grade while leaving the image accent highlights pure white. Shortening the pre-exposure will reduce the effect. With care you can calibrate this procedure for future use but be advised that the effect will change as the paper ages, and the test will have to be repeated for each paper type and grade you wish to use.

There is some danger that safelight fog may augment the pre-exposure. In fact, you may already be pre-flashing your paper without knowing it. You can check your safelight for safety by laying a strip of sensitized paper, about 2 inches × 8 inches, on your work table and covering half of it lengthwise with an opaque card. Leave it exposed to your normal safelight illumination for 2 or 3 minutes, or as long as paper would be uncovered during printing, then remove the card, turn out the safelights, and proceed with the pre-flashing test previously described. This allows you to compare the pre-exposure alone with the pre-exposure plus safelight fog, and you'll probably be surprised at the result. If your safelight is typical, you're likely to find it's contributing some pre-exposure to your prints, reducing their contrast and possibly causing veiled highlights. The effect is so subtle that it frequently goes unnoticed, but you'll see improved brilliance in your prints if you eliminate safelight fogging.

Here's another way to pre-flash paper for contrast control. Two foam plastic cups held over the enlarging lens will diffuse the light sufficiently to provide uniform exposure over the entire paper surface, even with the negative in place in the carrier. Test for optimum pre-flash exposure time as described in the text.

Paper Development Variations

Although papers are influenced much less by development variations than films are, print contrast can be controlled somewhat by varying developer strength and composition. Developing time changes are not very useful; prints must be developed for a certain minimum time to form maximum density, and extending developing time beyond that point affects density more than contrast.

Changes in developer concentration affect papers slightly but if the dilution is not extreme, papers develop to completion and image contrast is largely controlled by the inherent characteristic of the paper. The major effects are altered rate of development and, in some cases, a modification of image color. Extreme dilution, even with prolonged development times, typically results in reduced Dmax and a shift of image color toward brown or yellow.

Normal print developers are rather vigorous solutions, usually formulated with Metol and hydroquinone, or Phenidone and hydroquinone, and strongly activated with sodium carbonate or other potent alkaline salt. In these formulas the Metol or Phenidone tends to produce low-contrast images and the hydroquinone builds high contrast. The two types of reducing agents blended together produce "normal" contrast. If these ingredients are separated and mixed in individual solutions they can be blended in various proportions to produce a moderately contrasty effect, a moderately soft, low-contrast

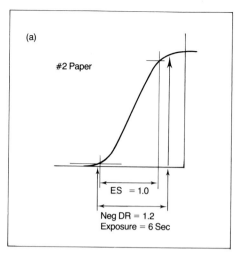

The negative used to make these prints has a density range of about 1.2. This illustrates the loss of highlight separation and opaque shadows that result when the negative is printed on "normal" paper whose ES is nominally 1.0. The figure above displays this relationship in graphic form; the negative range extends beyond both ends of the paper ES, placing some highlight tones on the extreme toe and running the dark tones off the curve shoulder.

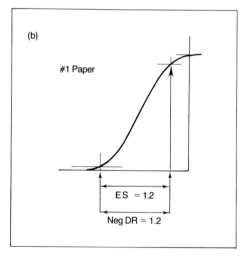

The print image is less harsh and has better detail in both tonal extremes when a softer paper is used, in this case contrast grade #1, whose ES is nominally 1.2 for this printing condition. Although this print is technically excellent, the reduced contrast and especially the lightened shadow tones have softened the visual effect, and made the brilliant sunlight appear slightly hazy. The figure above shows the paper curve and the negative DR placed properly for best exposure.

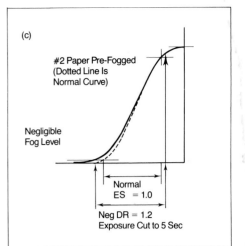

This print was made on the normal (#2) paper but the exposure was reduced slightly (5 seconds rather than 6) and the paper was pre-exposed to white light sufficiently to extend the paper curve toe. This treatment has resulted in good highlight detail and slightly more "open" shadows, while retaining the appearance of brilliant sunlight. Although this print expresses the feeling of the light, it is still too harsh and contrasty to be called good.

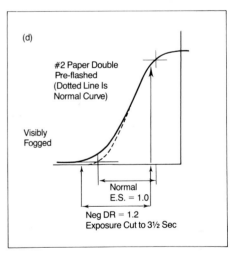

This print was also made on #2 paper but the pre-flash exposure was doubled and the print exposure reduced to 3½ seconds. These effects are shown graphically in the figure above. The slightly excessive pre-flash exposure has lengthened the curve toe and produced a perceptible fog density, while the reduced print exposure has shifted the negative DR to the left and placed the image shadow tones almost ideally on the curve, with only the black accents left on the shoulder. Visually the print approximates the highlight detail of a #1 paper with the shadow contrast of #2.

effect, or something in between. The venerable old "Dr. Beers" developer is one example. Here is one version of it:

Solution A:

Water	750.0 ml.
Metol (Elon)	8.0 gms.
Sodium sulfite (dessicated)	23.0 gms.
Sodium carbonate (monohydrated)	23.0 gms.
Potassium bromide	1.0 gm.
Add water to make	1.0 liter

Solution B:

Water	750.0 ml.
Hydroquinone	8.0 gms.
Sodium sulfite (dessicated)	23.0 gms.
Sodium carbonate (monohydrated)	32.0 gms.
Potassium bromide	2.5 gms.
Add water to make	1.0 liter

For use, appropriate volumes of each of the solutions are mixed with a quantity of water to form the working solution. The usual proportions are these:

Working Solution #	1	2	3	4	5	6	7
Parts of Solution A	8	7	6	5	4	3	2
Parts of Solution B	0	1	2	3	4	5	14
Parts of Water	8	8	8	8	8	8	0

Total Volume of Developer   16   parts

Number 4 mixture is presumably about "normal." Lower numbers give lower contrast; higher numbers, higher contrast, but the contrast range attainable depends on the paper type to a considerable extent. In tests run at Ohio State University, Blaine Moyer assembled these data:

Paper	Contrast Grade	Effective Exposure Scale			ES Range Beers
		Dektol	Beers #1	Beers #7	
Ilfobrom 3.IP	3	.77	.8	.68	.12
Brovira BS-111	3 (now 2)	.9	1.05	.98	.07
Portriga Rapid PRN-111	3 (now 2)	.95	1.02	.76	.26
Polycontrast	no filter	1.0	1.05	.92	.13
Polycontrast	#4	.7	.79	.62	.17

As might be expected, the Beers contrast range (ES range) is greatest for Portriga Rapid—a warm-tone chlorobromide emulsion—and least for Brovira—a fast, cold-tone paper. Since Portriga is presently available in only three rather widely spaced contrast grades, it's apparent that the Beers formula is useful for fine tuning print contrast on this paper. There is less advantage if you prefer Brovira and, if you are a Polycontrast user, you'll find it easier and neater to control contrast with the filters or your color head dichroics. It's worth remembering, though, that the Beers #7 solution provides more contrast than Dektol does, if you need more snap than the #4 filter produces.

Post-Treatment of Prints

The print curve can be modified, sometimes usefully, by treating the image with Farmer's Reducer. This is particularly effective for curing slight graying of the highlights but it must not be overdone. The action is likely to go too far if you aren't careful, leaving the print with glaring white blotches where the delicate highlights are supposed to be. Figure 12-7 shows the effect of reduction on a typical print curve.

The conventional intensification techniques that are effective with films are not as a rule applicable to prints. In most cases the image color is changed and the gain in Dmax is not significant. The print emulsion will respond to various bleach-and-re-development procedures but these techniques are more novel than practical for fine work in straight photography.

Toning is by far the most practical and effective method for increasing print Dmax and controlling the image color. Some toners also protect the silver image from deterioration by either "plating" it with,

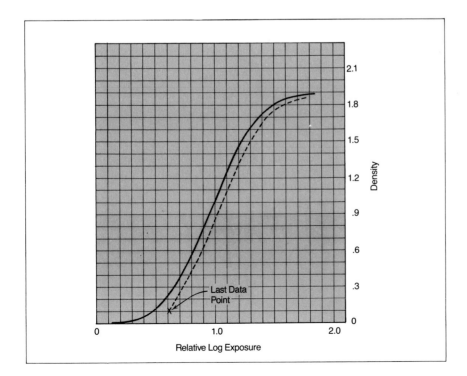

Figure 12-7. Farmer's reducer should be used with discretion on papers but it can be valuable for clearing grayed highlights. The broken line shows how reducer affects a paper curve.

or converting it to, a compound more stable than silver itself. Selenium toning is the most convenient and popular method for this purpose, but the gold protective toner is also effective on some papers. The initial effect is the same with both toners; the shadows appear to increase in depth and richness without obvious color change. If the toning is stopped at this point the image color change remains minimal when the print is dry; selenium produces a very slight warmth of tone and gold shifts the tone toward blue-black. As a rule warm-tone prints tone more quickly and strongly than cold-tone ones. Figure 12-8 shows the effects of gold and selenium protective toning on a typical printing paper.

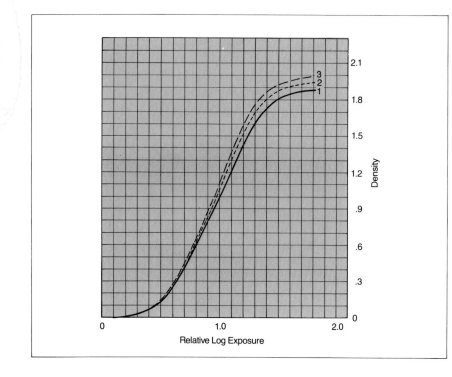

Figure 12-8. Toners are not equally effective on all papers, nor are all toners alike. These curves illustrate a normal Polycontrast curve (1), compared with similar curves toned with gold (2) and selenium (3). This demonstrates the effect of protective toning with only minor color change. Prolonged toning may actually lighten the blacks and reduce contrast if image color is changed significantly.

Toning, except as it affects Dmax, is not one of our concerns in this book, but a few general comments are probably appropriate. Prints to be toned should be treated in fresh fixer, preferably in two baths in sequence, for no longer than is necessary to insure complete removal of the unused silver salts. It's usually safe, and advisable, to leave the hardener out of the second bath. Following the fix, treat the prints without rinsing in a hypo clearing bath. Selenium toner concentrate can be added to the hypo clear if desired, but I prefer to use the toner as a separate solution. Dilute the concentrate with from about 9 to perhaps 30 parts water, and agitate the prints in this bath until there is an apparent intensification of the deep shadow tones. Then remove the prints from the toner before there is an appreciable change in image color. Toning will continue in the wash water for a little while, so don't overdo it.

Some photographers add a little hypo clearing bath concentrate, or sodium sulfite, or sodium metabrate to the toning solution though I have not found this necessary. If you have used plain water to mix the toner, the prints will wash more quickly and completely if they are treated with hypo clearing bath after toning. Then wash them thoroughly and dry them on screens.

Prints must be well washed before toning with gold. Pre-treatment in a real hypo-eliminator, such as Kodak's HE-1, and a thorough water wash is recommended. The toner can be made like this:

Solution A:

Water	100.0 ml.
Gold chloride	1.0 gm.

Solution B:

Water	1.0 liter
Sodium or potassium thiocyanate	20.0 gms.

For use, add about 10 ml. of solution A to 500 ml. of water and stir. Then add 500 ml. of solution B, stirring constantly. Use immediately. Toning should be sufficient to strengthen the blacks in from 1 or 2 to 10 minutes. Don't overdo it; the color change is very subtle and will be much more obvious when the print is dry. Agitate the print frequently to avoid uneven toning. It will be easier to judge the progress of the toning if you can compare the image with an identical untoned print soaking in plain water in an adjacent tray.

After several 8 × 10 prints have been treated and the toning action has slowed, additional gold can be added—with vigorous stirring—at the rate of about 2 or 3 ml. per print. Don't use too much gold solution. The toner is very expensive and it doesn't keep for more than an hour or so after the stock solutions have been mixed together. Rinse the toned prints in water, then treat them in hypo clearing bath again and wash thoroughly. Then dry them on screens.

Conclusion

The finished print represents the end of the process. It also brings us to the end of this book. I hope I've been able to persuade you that sensitometry has many practical applications and that it's not incomprehensible. Now it's up to you. If you've studied the concepts, followed the explanations of process, and plotted the curves carefully, you now have working data that can improve the quality and consistency of your negatives and prints. You can use these data or not, as you see fit, but even if you prefer not to use the exposure-development controls formally, your new knowledge should give you confidence and help you solve your technical problems intuitively.

Sensitometry isn't limited to testing materials for camera use, of course. You can use the procedures to test manufacturers' claims, confirm or refute the many popular myths and superstitions about the photographic process, or simply settle technical arguments with your friends. Is Brand X developer really able to produce higher effective film speed, better shadow detail, and more brilliant gradation than Brand Y? Can films really be "pushed" in development? Do compensating developers really work? Are modern papers incapable of producing good blacks? Does replenishment really maintain developer strength and activity at a uniform level? Are diffusion enlargers inherently superior (or inferior) to condenser enlargers? Does air drying prints produce better gradation and higher Dmax than heat drying? You can get objective answers to questions like these by following the test procedures you're now familiar with.

You can also apply these techniques to many darkroom procedures, with substantial savings in time and materials. For example, with step tablet and densitometer you'll find making balanced sets of separation negatives for dye transfer printing a relatively simple procedure. Similarly, you can produce tonal separations for posterization or line effects, and contrast-controlling masks for color printing or slide duplication, with predictable results and minimal waste.

You may be one of the growing number of photographers interested in the old processes such as gum bichromate, platinotype, kallitype, collotype, or photogravure. If so, you'll soon discover that making the necessary enlarged negatives or positives can be a haphazard, time-consuming process if done by trial and error. Your knowledge of sensitometry can streamline this operation and help you adjust the contrast and density of each negative for best results with the selected process. Perhaps even more importantly, in this era of fearfully expensive image metals, careful sensitometric testing can dramatically reduce waste of large sheet film and such precious raw materials as silver nitrate, platinum and palladium salts, uranyl nitrate, and gold chloride. This same controlled approach to photogravure and collotype can also save hours or days of work time and improve the quality of the finished plates.

In fact, if you're a serious photographer, interested in understanding and controlling the process, there's no good reason for *not* comprehending the principles of sensitometry and using them freely. Once you've given sensitometry a chance to work for you, I'm certain you'll agree.

Appendix

Determining Exposure Correction for Bellows Extension

The lens aperture calibrations—the f/ numbers—are derived from the lens focal length and the lens opening diameter:

$$f/ = \frac{\text{Focal length (F)}}{\text{Diameter (D)}}$$

When the lens is moved away from the film plane, as is necessary in focusing nearby objects, the distance between the film plane and the lens is referred to as the *focal distance* to distinguish it from the focal length. For practical work at any subject distance closer than infinity, therefore, the calibrated f/ numbers are not accurate and the formula should be written:

$$(\text{effective}) \ f/ = \frac{\text{Focal distance (FD)}}{\text{Diameter (D)}}$$

Throughout the normal working range, from a few feet from the camera to infinity, the focal distance is not significantly greater than the focal length but when the subject is less than about eight focal lengths from the camera, the difference becomes great enough to deserve attention. For example, if you are using a 4″ × 5″ view camera with its normal 6-inch (focal length) lens, to photograph an object 24 inches in front of the lens, you'll find—after focusing—the lens-to-film distance (focal distance) is about 8 inches:

$$\text{Focal distance} = \frac{\text{Subject distance} \times \text{Focal length}}{\text{Subject distance} - \text{Focal length}}$$

$$\text{or, FD} = \frac{24 \times 6}{24 - 6} = \frac{144}{18} = 8$$

If you have selected an aperture of f/16, the effective lens diameter is:

$$D = \frac{F}{f/} \quad \text{or} \quad \frac{6}{16} = .375 \text{ inches}$$

and the effective aperture is only:

$$f/ = \frac{FD}{D} \quad \text{or} \quad \frac{8}{.375} = 21.33 \text{ or about f/22}$$

To correct this, use the exposure time given for f/22, but leave the lens set on a marked aperture of f/16.

There are simpler ways to make this compensation. The method I prefer is this one: measure the focal distance; divide by the marked focal length; square the number and multiply the exposure time by it, like this:

> Focal distance is 8 inches
> Focal length is 6 inches
> The meter reads, say, 1 sec. @ f/16
>
> Necessary bellows factor $= \left(\dfrac{8}{6}\right)^2 = 1.78$
>
> Multiply shutter speed, $1 \times 1.78 = 1.78$

Set the lens on f/16 and expose for 1.78 seconds—about 2 seconds, practically speaking.

One convenient variation allows correction with the lens opening instead of exposure time. Using the same values in this formula:

$$\frac{\text{Focal distance}}{\text{Focal length}} = \frac{\text{Normal aperture}}{\text{Corrected aperture}}$$

$$\frac{8}{6} = \frac{16}{x} = 8x = 96 \quad \text{then, } x = 12 \text{ or f/12}$$

Set the lens at f/11 and use the 1-second exposure time.

Still another useful procedure is based on image magnification—the ratio of some dimension of the image compared with its corresponding subject dimension:

$$\text{Magnification} = \frac{\text{Image dimension}}{\text{Subject dimension}}$$

For example, if an image dimension measures ½ inch and the corresponding subject dimension measures 1½ inches, the magnification is:

$$\frac{0.5}{1.5} = 0.33$$

Then, the exposure increase factor is found by applying the formula:

$$\text{Exposure factor} = (\text{Magnification} + 1)^2$$

Then,

$$\text{Exposure factor} = (0.33 + 1)^2 = 1.33^2 = 1.77$$

Apply the factor to the shutter speed, as in the examples above.

There are other variations on these procedures. It doesn't matter how you arrive at the necessary exposure correction but you must make it somehow when using a lens at a focal distance significantly greater than its focal length. One caution: these formulas will not be entirely accurate for use with either telephoto or retrofocus lenses, such as may be fitted to 35mm SLRs. Since lenses of these types are not generally recommended for close-up work and since they are unlikely to be used with view cameras, they are not a concern of this book.

Printing Paper Characteristics

Brand Name of Paper	Contrast Grade	Useful DR	Condenser Enlarger (Tungsten) Curve Shape	SI	Cold Light Diffusion Enlarger Curve Shape	SI
Ilfobrom	0	0	2B	1.3		
	1	+	2B	1.15		
	2	+	1B	0.9	2B	1.15
	3	+	1C	0.75	2C	1.05
	4	+	1C	0.6		
	5	+	1C	0.5		
Portriga Rapid	1	++	3B	1.1	3C	1.55
	2	++	2B	0.95	3C	1.25
	3	++	1B	0.65	3C	0.9
Unicolor Exhibition	2	+	3C	1.2	4C	1.3
	3	+	2B	0.9	3B	1.0
Ilford Galerie	1	+	2C	1.35	3C	1.6
	2	+	2C	1.15	3D	1.35
	3	+	2B	0.8	3B	0.95
Polycontrast FB (filter)	1	0	1A	1.25		
	2	0	1B	1.0	3B	1.35*
	3	0	2B	0.85		
	4	0	2B	0.75		
Ilford Multigrade with Poly filter	2	0	1A	1.0	2B	1.25*
Ektamatic SC (in Dektol) with Poly filter	2	0	3B	0.8	3B	1.15*
Brovira	2	—	3D	1.1	4D	1.35

Key: Useful DR greater than 1.9 = ++
Between 1.9 and 1.8   = +
Between 1.8 and 1.7   = 0
Less than 1.7   = —

Curve Shape

Toe Contour	Shoulder Contour
1 Short	A Short
2 Medium	B Medium
3 Long	C Long
4 Very Long	D Very Long

Scale Index values are measured from Dmin (0.04-over-B + F) to a point on the curve where the gradient approximates 1.0. This gives greater SI values than the ANSI method does for most curves, but not for all. Paper characteristics vary considerably and can be altered by changes in chemicals and processing techniques. These data may not agree with your personal test results. For best accuracy, test your own.

* Tungsten Diffusion Enlarger.

In general terms the toe and shoulder contours of a paper curve describe image gradation. With some experience, you will be able to use curve information of this kind for creative purposes by matching individual negatives with papers that will interpret them most effectively.

There is no single "best" paper, nor is "normal" contrast paper necessarily ideal for all kinds of images. Curve shape (and therefore gradation) may be quite different for papers of different brand, grade, color, surface, and density range, even when the papers are matched with negatives of optimum contrast. Printing conditions introduce a similar set of variables: even with appropriately matching negatives, a given paper type, printed by contact, condenser projection, and diffusion projection, will produce visibly distinguishable images for each printing method. Again, there is no single "best" printing method. Each has its advantages and disadvantages. The choice is up to you.

Although both film and paper characteristics influence print gradation, the paper curve's effect is dominant. In general, a short-toe paper curve tends to separate the image light tones strongly and render subject mid-tones somewhat darker in the print than you might expect. Long-toe papers have the opposite tendency: light image tones are reduced in contrast while the subject mid-tones are rendered lighter than normal in the print image.

The shoulder contour effect is less obvious but still important. Short-shoulder papers tend to provide good shadow contrast down to near-black with an abrupt transition to solid black. Long-shoulder papers tend to reduce shadow contrast so that shadow details gradually merge into black but the lowered contrast may make the dark values appear veiled and lifeless.

The change in image contrast in both the toe and shoulder regions is most apparent in papers of short scale (high contrast). They typically tend to produce images of relatively low highlight and shadow contrast with harsh mid-tone gradation. Soft (long scale) papers, by comparison, generally produce more uniform gradation throughout the entire tonal range, which makes the inevitable loss of extreme highlight and shadow contrast seem less obvious.

For greatest image range, brilliance, and richness, it is obviously wise to select a paper (with a long density range) that can produce an intense black. This will permit you to print a satisfactorily long tonal scale without running into the curve shoulder and will insure good contrast in the deep shadow areas with emphatic black accents. The best papers for this purpose, in the list above, are those of + or ++ DR, with medium (B) shoulder contour. The worst choice is a paper of short DR and long shoulder—a combination that will practically guarantee weak, gray prints with opaque shadows.

Finally, remember that papers are less consistent and predictable than films are. They typically vary somewhat from box to box and their characteristics change gradually with age. In spite of these facts, I think you'll find these data interesting and useful as guides in the comparison and selection of papers for specific image needs.

Glossary

Arithmetic series: A sequence of numbers that progresses regularly by addition or subtraction of a constant.

ASA: American Standards Association, known since 1969 as the American National Standards Institute. ASA is commonly used to identify film speeds as determined by ANSI. See ISO.

Average gradient ($\overline{G}$): The slope of a line connecting two selected points on the film characteristic curve. The average gradient line can be shown to form the hypotenuse of a right triangle of which the base is the exposure range and the altitude is the density range. The value of average gradient is then determined by dividing the density range by the exposure range.

Base + Fog density: The density of a negative (or positive) resulting from all causes other than exposure to subject light. It includes the density of the film base material, the turbidity of the gelatin emulsion layer, traces of silver, residual dye stains, chemical fog, etc. When applied to paper prints, the term is generally considered to refer to the measurable reflection density of an unexposed area of the print, as compared to some white standard.

Bellows extension factor: A number expressing the reduction in film illumination which occurs when the lens-to-film distance is increased beyond the normal focal length, as in focusing on an object at close range.

Brightness: The subjective perception of luminance.

Characteristic curve: The graphic expression of the relationship between exposure values (charted on the x-axis) and density values (charted on the y-axis) as they are affected by development. Also sometimes called H & D curves after Ferdinand Hurter and Vero C. Driffield, who did the first serious analysis of these variables in the 1880s.

Compensating developer: A developer formulated or employed in such a way that it tends to limit mid-tone and highlight formation in the developing film image while allowing normal shadow development. The effect of compensating development, when it works, is to increase shadow contrast and minimize contrast in the higher values. Some developers for which compensating action is claimed merely produce a low-contrast image.

Condenser enlarger: A type of enlarger which employs one or more large plano-convex lenses to collimate the light from the lamp and converge it through the negative toward the image-forming lens. Condenser enlargers typically provide short printing times and produce relatively high-contrast images.

Constant: A fixed value in a calculation.

Contrast: That characteristic or combination of characteristics which makes things appear different from each other; usually refers to our perception of density differences in the image, especially the print image.

Density: Strictly, $Log_{10}O$—the common log of opacity, which is the reciprocal of transmittance. Loosely, the darkness of the image as measured with a densitometer.

Density range: Also sometimes called Density Scale; the difference between the extremes of density represented by an image; usually referring to the *useful* extremes.

Diffusion enlarger: A type of enlarger that illuminates the negative with nondirected light produced, typically, by a *cold-light* grid of gas-filled glass tubing, or by the illuminated interior of a matte white *integrating chamber*. The light from both sources may be further diffused by transmission through frosted glass or translucent plastic before reaching the negative. Diffusion enlargers typically produce low contrast images and minimize in the print the effects of minor blemishes contained in the negative.

Divided development: Process in which development is begun in one bath and completed in another. In water-bath development, the first solution is a normal developer, the second is plain water. In typical two-bath development the developer is split into its two usual components: the film is treated first in a solution containing the reducing agent and a preservative, then in a solution containing the accelerator, and perhaps a restrainer.

Dmax: Maximum density.

Dmin: Minimum density.

Exposure: (1) The act of allowing light to strike a sensitized surface. (2) The invisible effect on a sensitized surface, caused by allowing light to strike it. (3) The product of exposure time and light intensity.

Exposure range (ER): The difference between the greatest and the least exposure given to a film or paper emulsion. Similar to Exposure Scale (ES). Usually refers to the difference between the *useful* extremes of exposure.

Flare: Nonimage light that reaches the film in the camera, typically caused by light diffused or reflected by the lens surfaces, or by reflections from bright surfaces on the lens mount or camera interior. It may show up as a distinct pattern or as general fog.

Flat: An image that is low in contrast.

Fog: (1) The act of exposing a sensitized surface to nonimage-forming light. (2) The effect of exposure to nonimage-forming light, as evidenced by a general reduction of image contrast, and either general or local increase in density unrelated to image density. *Light fog* is sometimes distinguished from *chemical fog*, a density produced by chemical action on the emulsion, unrelated to exposure.

Gamma: The tangent of the acute base angle in the right triangle formed by extending the straight-line portion of the characteristic curve to intersect the exposure axis (base) and the density axis (altitude) of the graph. The numerical value is found by dividing the Density Range by the Subject Brightness Range.

Geometric series: A sequence of numbers that progresses regularly by multiplication or division by a constant.

Gradation: The visual progression of image tones from light to dark or dark to light.

Gradient (G): The angle or slope of a portion of the characteristic curve.

Gross fog: Same as base-plus-fog.

Illuminance: The measurable light in the subject space or falling on the subject surfaces.

Incident light: Light falling on the subject or existing in the subject space; illuminance.

Intermittency effect: The reduced efficiency of multiple, accumulated exposure increments as compared with a single exposure of equivalent total duration.

ISO: International Organization for Standardization; also a film speed standard, proposed by ISO and now accepted by the industry, which replaces the older ASA standard and European standards. In effect the ISO standard simply recognizes existing ASA (American) and DIN (German) speeds; for example, a film previously rated ASA 100 or 21 DIN now carries the designation ISO 100/21°.

Latent image: The invisible effect of light exposure on a sensitized material; development makes the latent image visible.

Logarithm: In the common system, an exponent of the base number 10, representing the power to which 10 must be raised to produce a given number. Other base numbers can be used. Abbreviated as log or log_{10}.

Log exposure: Also written logE or logH; a numerical value of exposure expressed as a logarithm.

Luminance: The measurable light emitted by, transmitted through, or reflected from the subject surfaces.

Luminance meter: An exposure meter used for measurement of luminance.

Meter-candle-second (mcs): A standard unit of exposure, equivalent to that produced in one second by the light from a "standard candle" (a light source simulating the intensity and color of the light from solidifying molten platinum) one meter away from a sensitized surface. Lux-second is a similar term.

Negative: An image whose tones are reversed from those of the original subject; usually refers to a film image in which the subject lights are recorded as dark tones, and vice versa.

N-number: In the Zone System, a number expressing in stops the difference between some specified portion of the ideal subject range and a similar portion of the range of a real subject, as measured with a meter. If the measured range is greater than the ideal, the N-number is a minus number; if less, it's a plus number.

One-shot developer: A developer solution used once, then discarded.

Positive: An image whose tones resemble those of the original from which it was made; the conventional print image is a positive (negative of the negative) because it resembles the original subject in tonality.

Pre-visualization: As commonly used by Zone System workers, the act of comparing an idealized mental image of the subject with the subject itself (before making the camera exposure) as a guide in selecting appropriate values of exposure and development; visualization.

Reciprocity failure: The effective loss of sensitivity and change in contrast of a film or paper emulsion when the exposing light is of either very high or very low intensity.

Reflectance meter: Same as luminance meter.

Reflection density: Density measured by reflected light.

SBR: Subject Brightness Range; in this book these initials are used to stand for Subject *Luminance* Range (a preferable term) to avoid confusion with Single Lens Reflex (SLR).

Scale index (SI): A term used to indicate a personalized value of print Exposure Scale (ES).

Shoulder: The portion of a characteristic curve beyond the straight-line portion, characterized by a decrease in gradient as exposure is increased.

Speed: In reference to sensitized materials, sensitivity.

Speed point: On a characteristic curve, a selected reference point used in determining the relative speed of films or papers. The ASA standard speed point is found on the film curve at a density level of 0.1 over B + F; for papers the standard density level is 0.6 over B + F.

Step: A term sometimes used to denote a change in exposure or density by a factor of 2. In this book, the term refers to any increment in a series of exposure or density values, regardless of the interval or value represented.

Stop: (1) The lens opening or aperture. (2) In this book, and in general usage, a change in exposure (and occasionally density) by a factor of 2, from any cause.

Straight-line portion: The section of a characteristic curve between toe and shoulder, characterized by its uniform gradient.

Subject luminance range: The difference between the *measured* extremes of subject luminance, as distinct from Subject Brightness Range, which, strictly speaking, refers to the *visible* difference between the tonal extremes. Abbreviated, in this book, SBR.

Toe: The lower extremity of the characteristic curve, identified by an increase in gradient as exposure is increased.

Transmission density: Density as measured by transmitted light.

Value: (1) Amount, quantity or magnitude; as, a value of exposure. (2) Also, in this book, used as artists use the term in the Munsell system of color notation, to refer to the lightness or darkness of a tone or color, without respect to its hue.

X-axis: The horizontal axis of a graph; the exposure axis of the characteristic curve graph.

Y-axis: The vertical axis of a graph; the density axis of the characteristic curve graph.

Zone: An ambiguous term. In this book, any one of the several divisions of the print gray scale which represent separate, consecutive luminance ranges of 1 stop in the normal subject. In subjects of other than the normal 7-stop range, each print zone represents $1/7$ of the total SBR, whatever it is. Print zones stand for specific average values of gray which when memorized assist the photographer in visualization.

Answers to the Exercises in Chapter 2

1. The numbers are 50 and 72. In this sequence every second number is doubled (the constant is the square root of 2, or about 1.41).

2. You should use f/5.6. The factor of 8x is equivalent to 3 stops—from f/16 to f/11 (1); f/11 to f/8 (2); f/8 to f/5.6 (3).

3. The luminance ratio is 256:1. Count 8 stops on your fingers: 2, 4, 8, 16, 32, 64, 128, 256. Alternatively, use your calculator to raise 2 to the 8th power (2^8) by keying 2, then y^x, then 8, then =, to get the answer: 256. A third alternative: multiply the number of stops (8) by the log equivalent of 1 stop (log of 2 is 0.3) and take the antilog: $8 \times 0.3 = 2.4$; the antilog of 2.4 is approximately 256 (actually 251.18864 if done on a calculator, but that's close enough). If you do the whole calculation on a calculator, using a more accurate value of the log of 2 (0.30103) you'll get 2.40824, for which the antilog is 256.00002—very close indeed.

4. Beginning with 2 seconds, the times are: 2, 2.8, 4, 5.6, 8, 11, 16, and 22 seconds. Does this sequence look familiar? It should; the constant is the square root of 2 (1.41), just as in the f-number sequence.

5. Its ISO rating is 100/21° and you would set your meter at ASA 100 to use it. The DIN numbers are in log sequence with the decimal point omitted, that is, DIN 22 stands for 2.2 and DIN 26 stands for 2.6. Since each log interval of 0.1 equals 1/3 stop, and the ASA numbers also progress by 1/3 stop increments, the two systems relate like this:

ASA	DIN
50	18
64	19
80	20
100	21
125	22
160	23
200	24
250	25
320	26
400	27, etc.

6. Use an ND 2.0 filter. The log of 100 is 2.0.

7. The intensity must be reduced by 5 stops and the ND filter value is ND 1.5. Count through the aperture number sequence to find the number of stops: f/8 to f/11 (1 stop); 11 to 16 (2); 16 to 22 (3); 22 to 32 (4); 32 to 45 (5 stops); then since each stop is equivalent to a log interval of 0.3, multiply 5 × 0.3 to find the ND value, 1.5. Alternatively, divide f/45 by f/8 and square it to find the exposure ratio represented:

$$\frac{45}{8} = 5.625 \qquad 5.625^2 = 31.64, \text{ or about } 32$$

The ND value is equal to the log of the exposure ratio:

$$\log \text{ of } 32 = 1.5$$

8. Fifty units of light will pass through. Count off $4\frac{1}{3}$ stops on your fingers (equivalent to a log range of 1.3): 1000 to 500 (1); 500 to 250 (2); 250 to 125 (3); 125 to 64 (4); 64 to *50* (this is $\frac{1}{3}$ of a stop, just as it is in the ASA number series). Alternatively, since 500 is 0.3 less than 1000, and the filter value, 1.0, allows only $\frac{1}{10}$ of the light to pass (divides the light by 10), 500 divided by 10 is 50. A third alternative: find the log of 1000 (3.0), subtract the total filter value (1.3) which gives 1.7. The antilog of 1.7 is 50.

9. You need ND 2.6. Divide 2000 by 5 to get 400. The log of 400 is 2.6. Alternatively, subtract the log of 5 (0.69897) from the log of 2000 (3.30103) to get 2.60206, which approximates the filter value, 2.6.

10. You must develop for about 2 minutes for a CI of .45. If you develop for 3 minutes you'll reach a CI of about .525.

Index